Two Legged Snakes

Two Legged Snakes

Understanding and Handling Manipulative People

Dr. Ed Slack

Simple Truth Publishing

Two Legged Snakes: Understanding and Handling Manipulative People
by Dr. Ed Slack

Simple Truth Publishing books may be purchased for educational, business, or sales promotional use. For information, please write: Special Markets Department, Simple Truth Publishing, P.O. Box 292828, Nashville TN 37229 USA

Disclaimer: No references or illustrations in this book are intended to represent any actual person or event, except when specifically noted.

First Edition

Publisher's Cataloging-In-Publication Data
(Prepared by The Donohue Group, Inc.)

Slack, Ed (Edward G.)
  Two legged snakes : understanding and handling manipulative people / Ed Slack. -- 1st ed.

    p. : ill. ; cm.

  Includes bibliographical references.
  ISBN-13: 978-0-9825514-1-7
  ISBN-10: 0-9825514-1-X

1. Manipulative behavior. 2. Control (Psychology) 3. Interpersonal relations.
I. Title.

BF632.5 .S53 2010
158.2   2009939075

Designed by Patrick Schlafer
www.pschlafer.com

Copy edit and proofreading by Ms. Gail Kearns
www.topressandbeyond.com

Printed in China

This book is dedicated to all the people who read it and put it to good use.

Thanks for making the world a less snaky place.

The Parts

1   Introduction

2   Two Legged Snakes: What They Are

14   Why Two Legged Snakes Have Become Such a Problem

23   Types of Two Legged Snakes

The Charmer • The Backstabber • The Bombast Entertainer • The Bilker • The Decorated • The Misdirector • The Rhetorical • The Situational • The Media Maven • The Lost • The Lifer • The Justified • The King Cobra • The Transcendents

41   The Apple Biters: Types of Two Legged Snake Fans

The True Believer • The WannaBe • The Follow the Leader • The Loyalists

50   Common Two Legged Snake
       Persuasive Techniques
           Accusination • Misdirection •
           Misassociation • Going Big •
           Disproportioning • Rave-Up Questioning •
           Burlesquing • Bombasting • Viperation •
           Overtalking • Demanding • Begging
           Sympathy • Flattery • Yes Setting •
           Reinventing History

70   Two Legged Snake Biting Styles
           The Nibbler • The Chomper • The Pouncer

75   Handling Two Legged Snakes
           Relationships and Two Legged Snakes •
           Family and Familiars • The Ladder of
           Friendship • Bipedal Snake Experts

98   The Snakes in Our Heads

108   Illustration and Design Team

110   Bibliography

111   Two Legged Snake Spotters Checklist

Introduction

Who and what we trust is an automatic and for most, a largely unexamined process. We receive thousands of messages each day, tugging at us to buy this, believe that, and support this or that view. Contrary to all these choices is the fact that most people know little about how to decipher the false from the true, the manipulative from the sincere, and the ill-advised from the functional. This gap was the motivation for writing *Two Legged Snakes: Understanding and Handling Manipulative People.*

I began writing in the usual academic manner but Shel Silverstein's *The Missing Piece Meets the Big O* kept coming to mind. Hundreds of times during my years as a psychologist, I've reached for my well-worn copy and had clients leaf through it. In five minutes, this short illustrated book got across points about relationship dynamics that often took hours of expensive talk. Its words and pictures told the simple truth in a humorous and memorable style. I was inspired to take a new approach.

Using words and pictures together causes the reader to use more of his or her brain than text alone. In technical terms, this is called multi-modal processing, and it has been shown to help many people understand and remember more effectively, particularly those of us with a touch of dyslexia or a bit of ADD. Our topic, though quite serious, is approached in the lighthearted manner inspired by Mr. Silverstein, who proved that meaningful books don't have to be a words-only experience and can be fun as well.

ES

Two Legged Snakes: What They Are

The greatest single factor determining your level of happiness and success is who you listen to and who you trust. Even if you have been fortunate to grow up in an environment surrounded by functional, trustworthy people, you are still not safe from those who actively use deception, rhetorical techniques, and symbolic manipulation to cause you to act against your own best interests. Every day the goal of Two Legged Snakes is to get into your wallet, get into your pants, and get into your head. They will sell you things you don't need, break your heart, steal from you with a smile, and garner your support for agendas that benefit them at ridiculous costs to you.

Although Two Legged Snakes currently come in more varieties then ever before, they aren't a new problem. According to Christian, Islamic and Jewish traditions, man's first decision-making responsibilities began with Eve letting herself get talked into eating the fruit of the Tree of Knowledge; the one fruit she was forbidden by God to eat.

Why did she do it? She had it made living in the Garden of Eden (a very nice place). She was living with Adam (a great guy by most accounts), all her needs were tended to, she lived in peace with all God's creatures and she had eternal life. Why would she eat the forbidden fruit and then share it with Adam and get them both kicked out of paradise? Because a serpent talked her into it. She was tempted and gave in to snaky manipulation. And this serpent, by many reputable accounts, walked on two legs. Even if you're not a religious person, every day you face the same dilemma Eve faced:

To bite or not to bite, that is the question.

It makes sense that major world religions would put this story at the forefront of their traditions. It highlights one of our most important tasks as human beings: to choose well and not be deceived by snaky influences. If we are to do our best to avoid the pitfalls and disasters that are the results of poor decisions, we must learn the techniques and appearances of those who would manipulate us and make our choices clear of their influence. We need to be aware of Two Legged Snakes and their methods.

All of us have a snaky side and we've all heard its voice trying to influence us. But our general intent is to resolve problems fairly and treat others as we'd like to be treated. Being imperfect, we slip up sometimes.

And then we feel really bad, say we're sorry and honestly try to do better next time. Our family life, work life and relationships going well are what's important, not the snaky pursuits of janky affairs, deceived loved ones and ill gotten gains. Two Legged Snakes commonly deceive their partners simply for the feeling of power they get from not getting caught.

Bipedal Snakes can be charming, talented, entertaining, attractive and above all, persuasive. Even though it's often hard to believe, their focus is to achieve their snaky goals no matter what. The resulting consequences range from personal discomfort to international disaster.

A BS boyfriend or girlfriend will use you for sex or money, dump you when it suits them and often leave you with unwanted medical issues. BS mechanics charge way too much for what you didn't need anyway. BS doctors recommend unnecessary and expensive procedures that frequently leave you with a new and worse set of problems. BS religious and political leaders cause many types of disasters. The bombing of the Twin Towers on 9-11, the state sanctioned massacre of 800,000 Tutsis in Rwanda and Joseph Stalin's paranoia fueled genocide of seven million Russians are a few of this century's leading examples of how bad things can get when Two Legged Snakes lead the show.

There are two basic categories of Two Legged Snakes: Primary and Secondary. Most Primaries are created by psychological reactions to negative social experience, combined with certain natural abilities. This recipe usually starts with a painful, self-image damaging trauma that is covered by a memory fugue (forgetting or repressing the trauma). That creates an unconscious conflict that is then compensated for with the behaviors and attributes the budding Bipedal Snake is most gifted with.

Picture a little boy cruelly and repeatedly taunted by his playmates and family members because they say he isn't good at art. This is the trauma part.

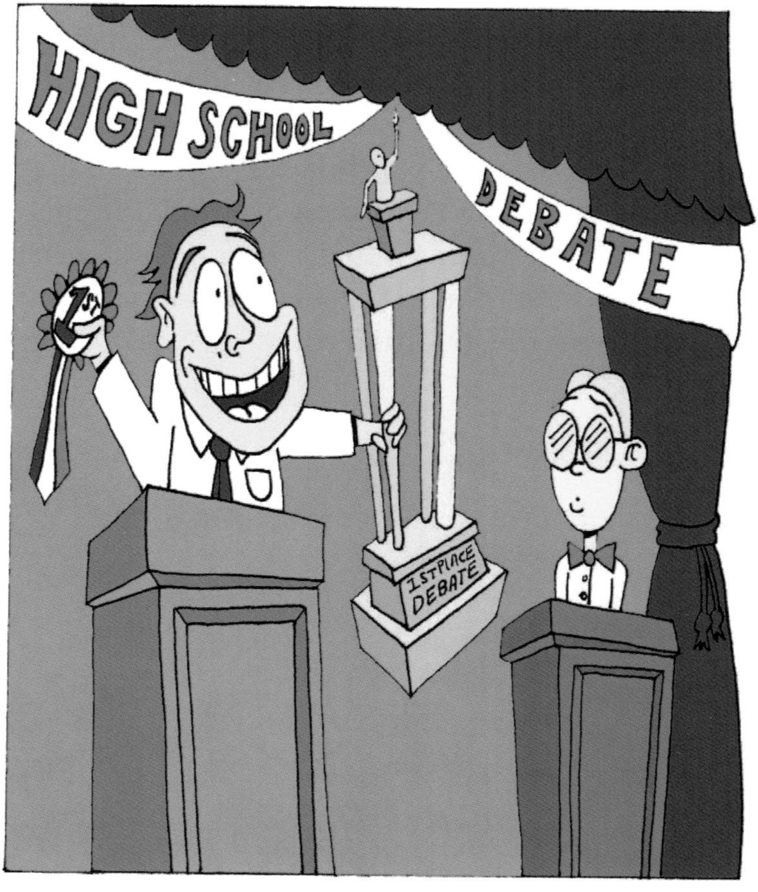
HIGH SCHOOL
DEBATE
1ST
1ST PLACE
DEBATE

As he gets older he discovers he has a gift for argument and social tactics (talent) and that he can use this to get over on people, better his social standing and win, win, win. This newly found power is much enjoyed.

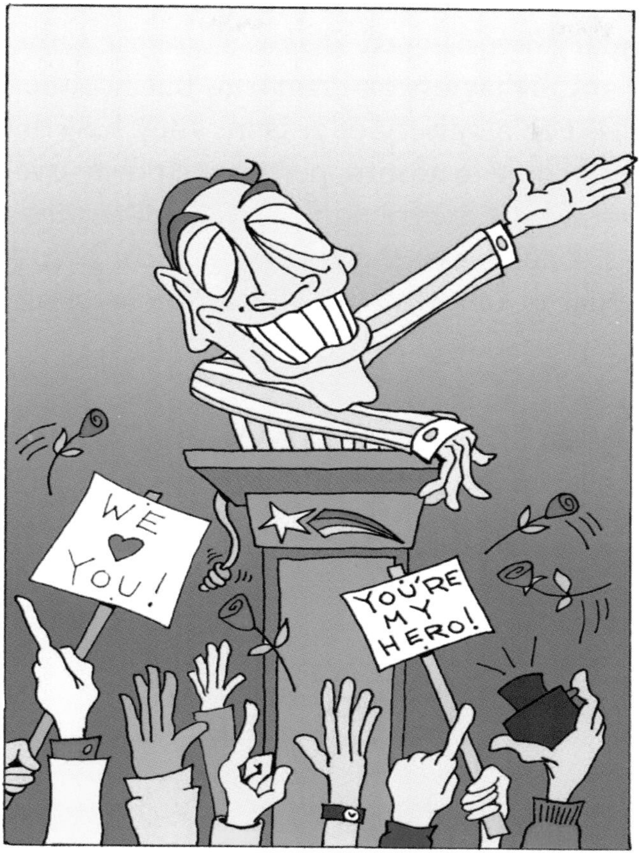
WE ♥ YOU!
YOU'RE MY HERO!

Though he's not sure why he's more driven than his peers to gather popularity and win on the rhetorical battlefield (memory fugue), it sure feels good (compensation). There are unlimited variations, but that's the general pattern.

Secondary Two Legged Snakes share the same talents, tactics and behaviors as Primaries but not the internal conflicts. For a variety of reasons they have bitten the apple and come to admire persuasive power over honest endeavor. Many are friendly, well-liked, family-oriented people. Nonetheless, their value of form over function and denial of objective reality can be as dangerous as boating with 'snaky expert' Captain Dave.

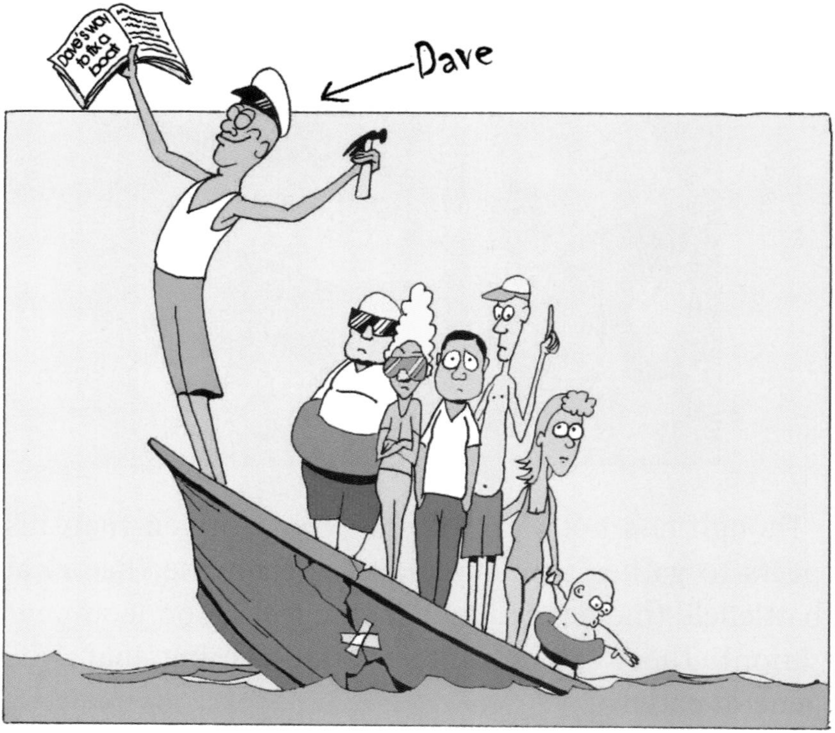
Dave's way to fix a boat
Dave

When we begin to see how much snaky behavior goes on in the world, it can be a pretty depressing realization. It's important to remember that both types of snakes are usually unaware that they are operating under the influence of dysfunctional psychological principles. In fact, many feel they have high moral standards. This phenomenon is even more pronounced in Two Legged Snakes who are compelled to take their compensations to the public level. In this realm the wider breadth of influence offers an enhanced ability to cover their unconscious conflicts with amplified feelings of justification and validation. This public forum additionally provides the opportunity, on a grand scale, to manipulate a population by playing on their insecurities and emotions. BSs offer solutions to people who are doubtful, stubborn, fearful or angry, that promise near instant gratification and that often end in disaster. Remember the young art house flop in 1920's Germany, who had a talent for propaganda and an arsenal of compensatory hate?

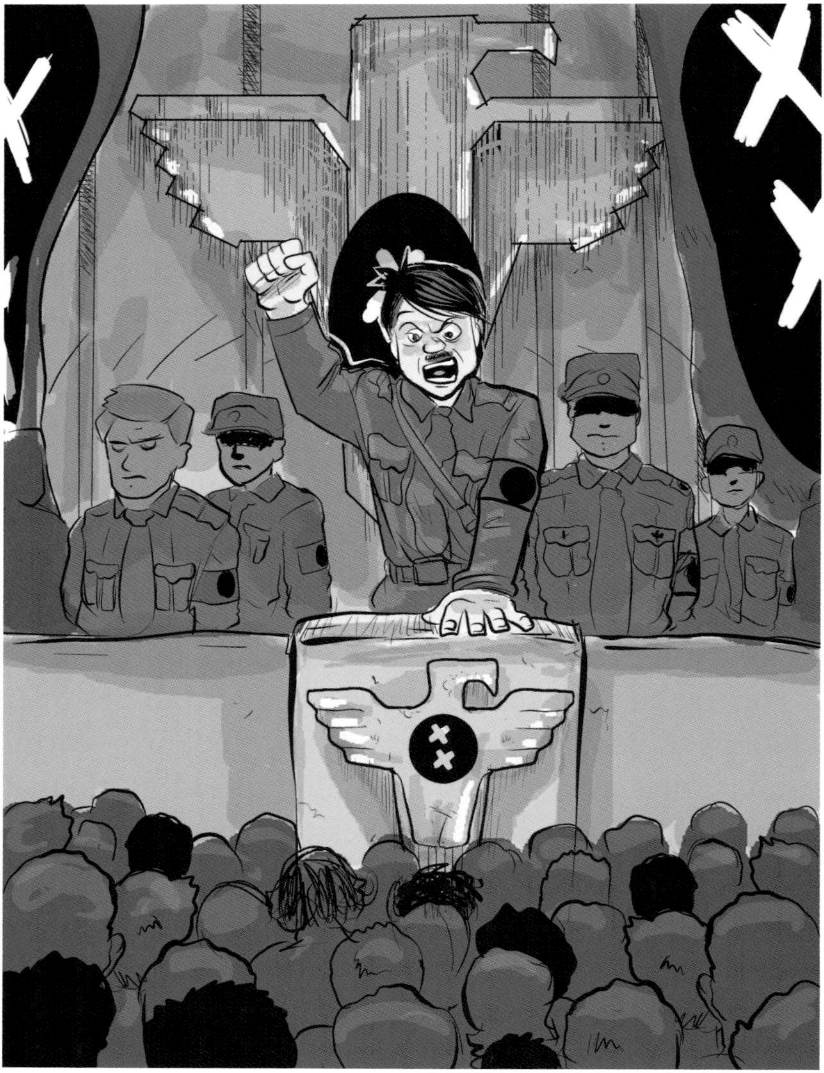

The freedom you are fortunate to enjoy gives you the ability to make decisions about virtually every aspect of your life. Every day BSs try to use this freedom to get into your wallet, your heart and your head. With so many Two Legged Snakes about, our freedom comes with the responsibility to be snake aware. A BS influenced romantic disaster or investment decision will be devastating on a personal level. An apple biting vote or campaign contribution, which may seem like a small thing, will have consequences and repercussions that last for years and years and affect a huge number of people.

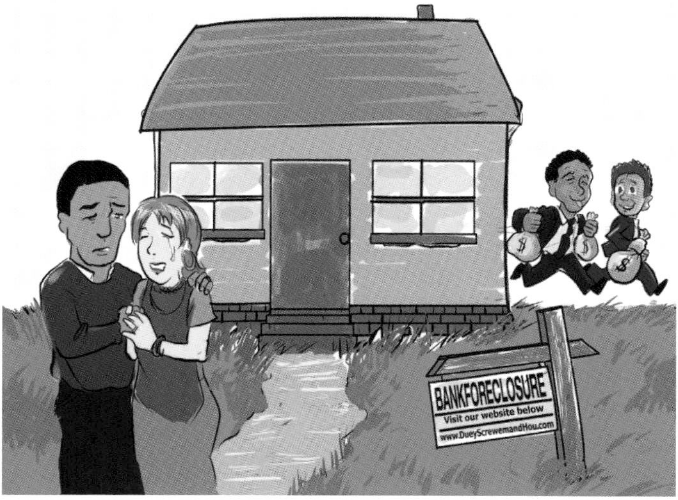
BANKFORECLOSURE
Visit our website below
www.DueyScrewemandHou.com

Why Two Legged Snakes Have Become Such a Problem

Certain environmental conditions favor the growth of a particular species or subspecies, even those that are not good for the population as a whole. The factors that have encouraged the current overgrowth of the Two Legged Snake population fall into three main areas:

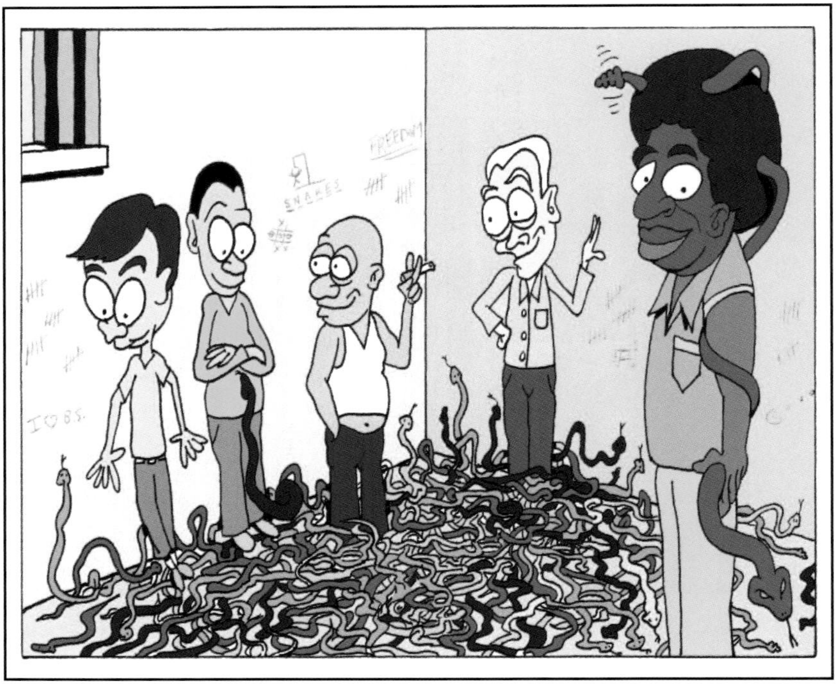
SNAKES

Lack of awareness.

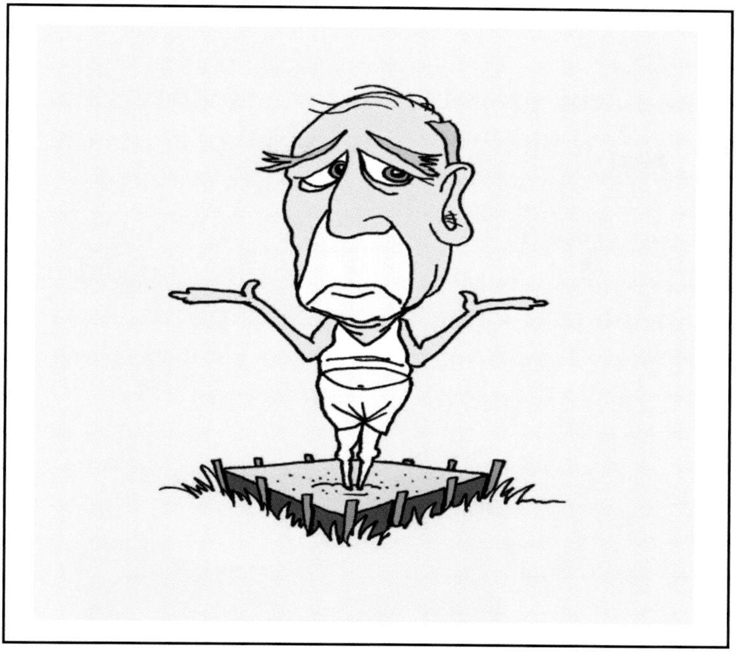

Aversion to change.

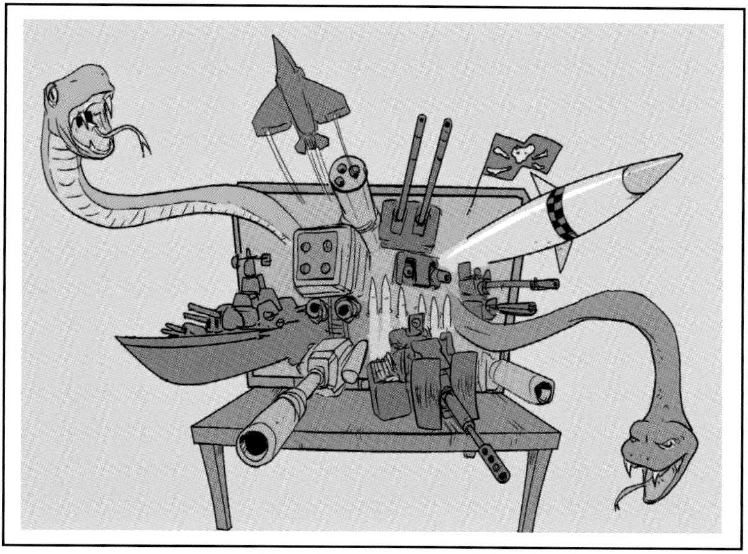

And powerful propaganda.

A significant proportion of our society values the theater of persuasive ability, symbolic rhetoric and charismatic appeal over the reality of observed behavior, intelligent analysis and decision making that's concerned with what actually works. Bipedal Snakes have an internal value system that prizes social validation over function, prevalence over wisdom, and rhetoric over truth. For BSs, BS is king.

Would you choose a surgeon based solely on their looks? If the brakes on your car need repair are you more concerned with the repair shop's color scheme or reputation? Would you prefer a charming investment advisor of unknown abilities or a socially awkward one with a stellar track record? Two Legged Snakes would have you believe that how something appears (its form) is representative of how well something works (its function). This is rarely the case. A snake expert may be able to win an argument about boat repair but in reality will probably be poor at actually repairing boats. If you want to know who knows what, look at their record, not how flashy their sign is.

Snaky advertising and persuasion tug at us thousands of times a day, and many of the techniques used are powerful. There are laws designed to protect us from these types of attacks but they are few and for the most part ineffective or unenforced. However, anyone who has a basic awareness of the ways and means of snaky sophistry is largely protected from having their heads and hearts filled with BS directives, perspectives, opinions, and ideas.

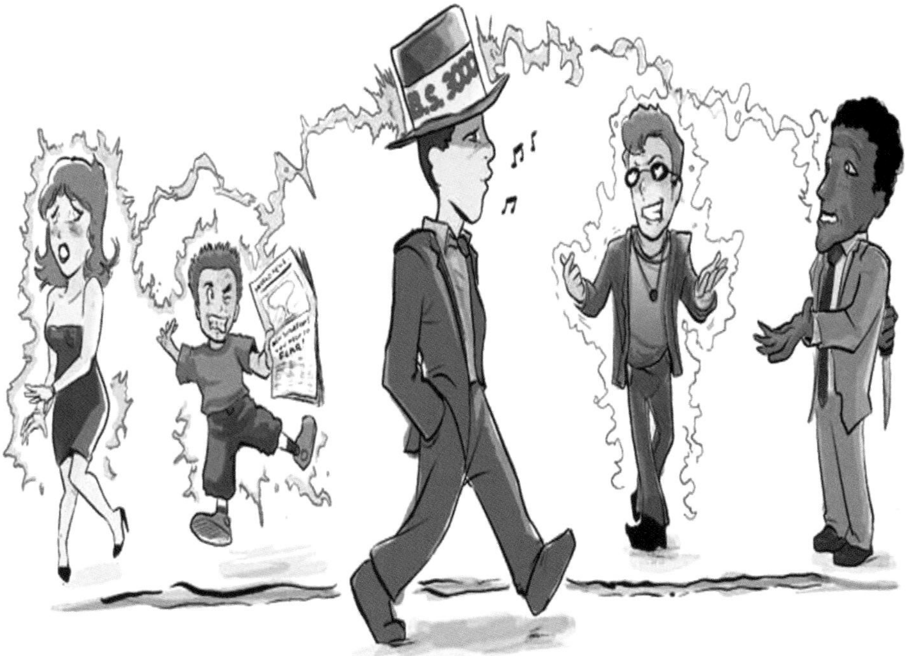
B.S. 3000

The rate of change in our social lives is currently at an all-time high. This is challenging for a species that has enjoyed a much slower rate for the vast majority of its existence. Methods of communication, family roles and dynamics, social standards, styles, sexual attitudes, religious beliefs, political perspectives, etc., are all in flux. Many don't want this inevitable growth and requisite change. Alvin Toffler in his seminal book, *Future Shock*, states, "the more change threatens from without, the more meticulously reversionists repeat past modes of action. Their social outlook is regressive and unrealistically supportive of a return to the glories of yesteryear." Others who are resistant to change don't operate from a perspective of fear but are simply unquestioningly loyal to traditional values and perspectives or just plain like things how they are and don't pay much attention to politics. Nonetheless, Two Legged Snakes direct this change-averse population with assurances, symbols and rhetoric that exemplify the values of the past and a comforting 'keep the status quo' stance. The ability to manipulate this huge population gives BSs enormous power in the political arenas.

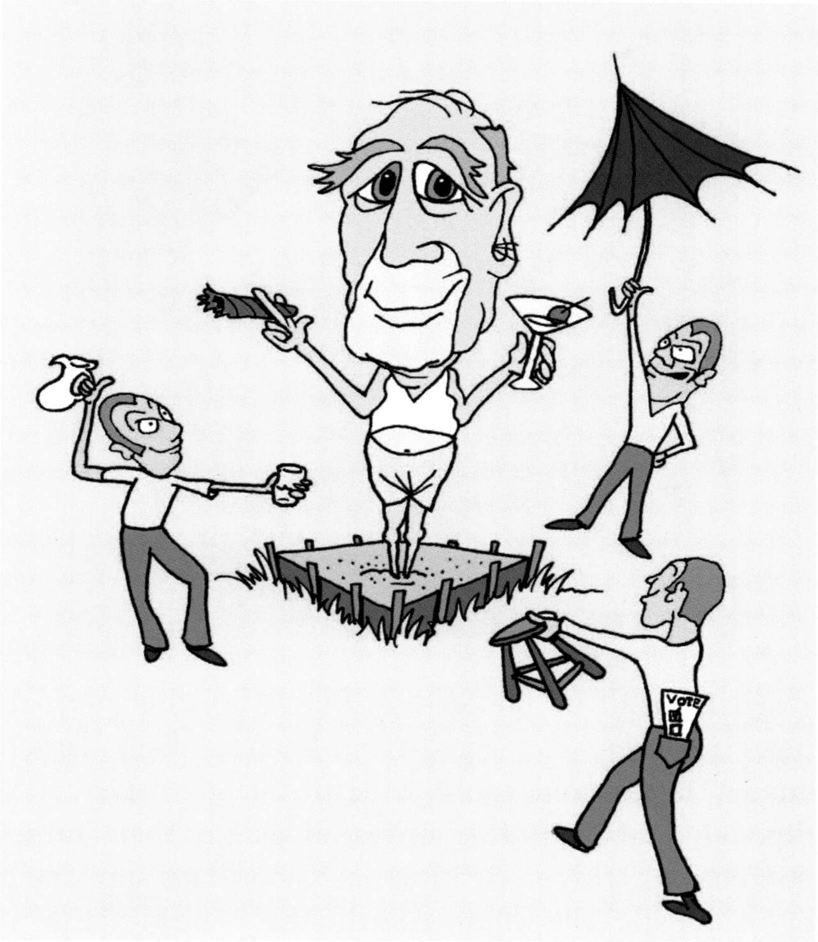
VOTE

Media on all its platforms—TV, radio, the internet, news services, etc.—has an influence that's larger, louder, faster, and more widespread than ever. The Bipedal Snakes in this arena focus on their target populations with a scientific precision that's supported by sophisticated and coordinated multi-platform staging and dazzling special effects. It's the best looking, best sounding, most convincing BSing of all time.

Flashy presentation isn't the only reason media has enhanced BS power. Not long ago, it was the standard for journalists to see their jobs as a calling: to report the truth and be a watchful force protecting the public. Ironically, that force now typically uses snaky persuasive techniques, such as sensationalizing, misdirecting, and disproportioning to keep viewership numbers and ad revenues high. When profit becomes more important than truth, the snakes come marching in.

Unless Irish snake removal expert St. Patrick makes himself available for another snake drive, the cure for this epidemic is for us to learn how to identify Two Legged Snakes, be aware of their techniques, and develop our snake handling skills.

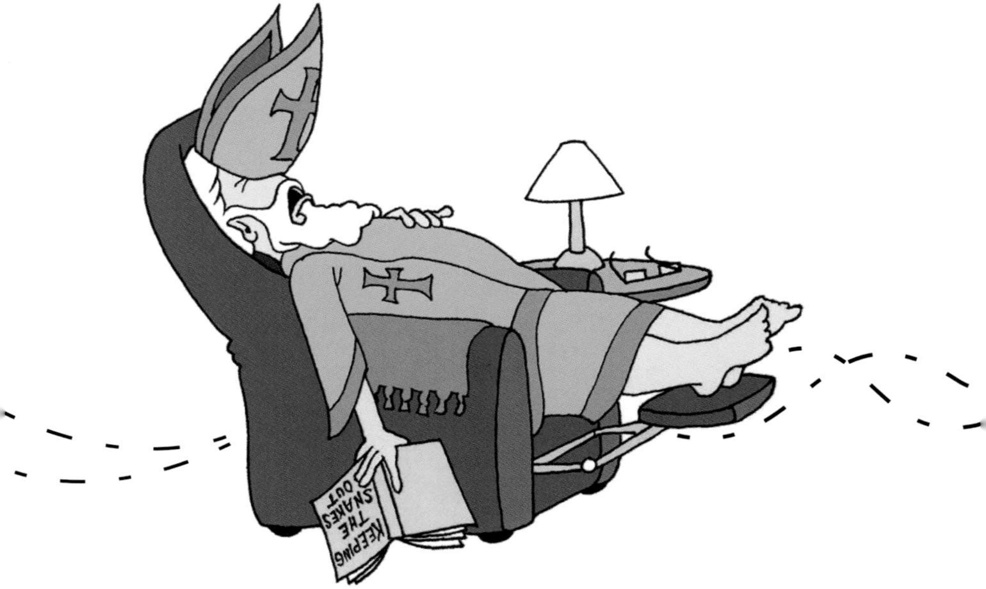
KEEPING THE SNAKES OUT

If you want to be as free as possible from Two Legged Snake manipulations, you need to think for yourself and not be dependent on others opinions, learn to honestly see cause and effect and memorize the basic BS types and techniques. Doing this you will have immunized yourself from snaky sophistry.

Types of Two Legged Snakes

Besides Primary and Secondary, Two Legged Snakes are classified into two further, general categories: Day to Day (D2D) and Public Level Bipedal Snakes (PBS). D2D's are those we come in contact with during normal daily activities: doctors, teachers, mechanics, salespeople, and so forth. PBSs operate on the viewable stage, where their influence is felt, on varying levels, by virtually everyone on the planet. PBSs typically work in concert with other snakes and use BS fans, or Apple Biters, who act to further their cause.

Memorizing the basic types of Two Legged Snakes is a great idea because it helps you cluster large amounts of information around a central theme (the snake or snake fan type). This frees up your brain and as a result you're smarter and more aware.

THE CHARMER: This Bipedal Snake is very aware of social standards. Found on both levels, Charmers are charismatic and usually have a role of some importance or at least one that looks good. Whether they are political big wigs or a High School Principal, the ruse is the same: They use their attributes and position as a symbolic cloak to make the snaky things they do seem implausible. When exposed, Public Level Charmers are often protected by a die-hard fan base that believes in their cult of personality no matter what. Charmers know no shame and will lie without conscience, even associating themselves with revered people and events they in no way resemble. They are fairly easy to spot if you check the differential between how they present themselves and the reality of what they've actually done or know. Typically not the brightest bulbs on the snaky chandelier, Charmers often get manipulated by brighter BSs. Even so, this is a dangerous type as they are adept at getting into positions of power or intimacy and then causing disaster.

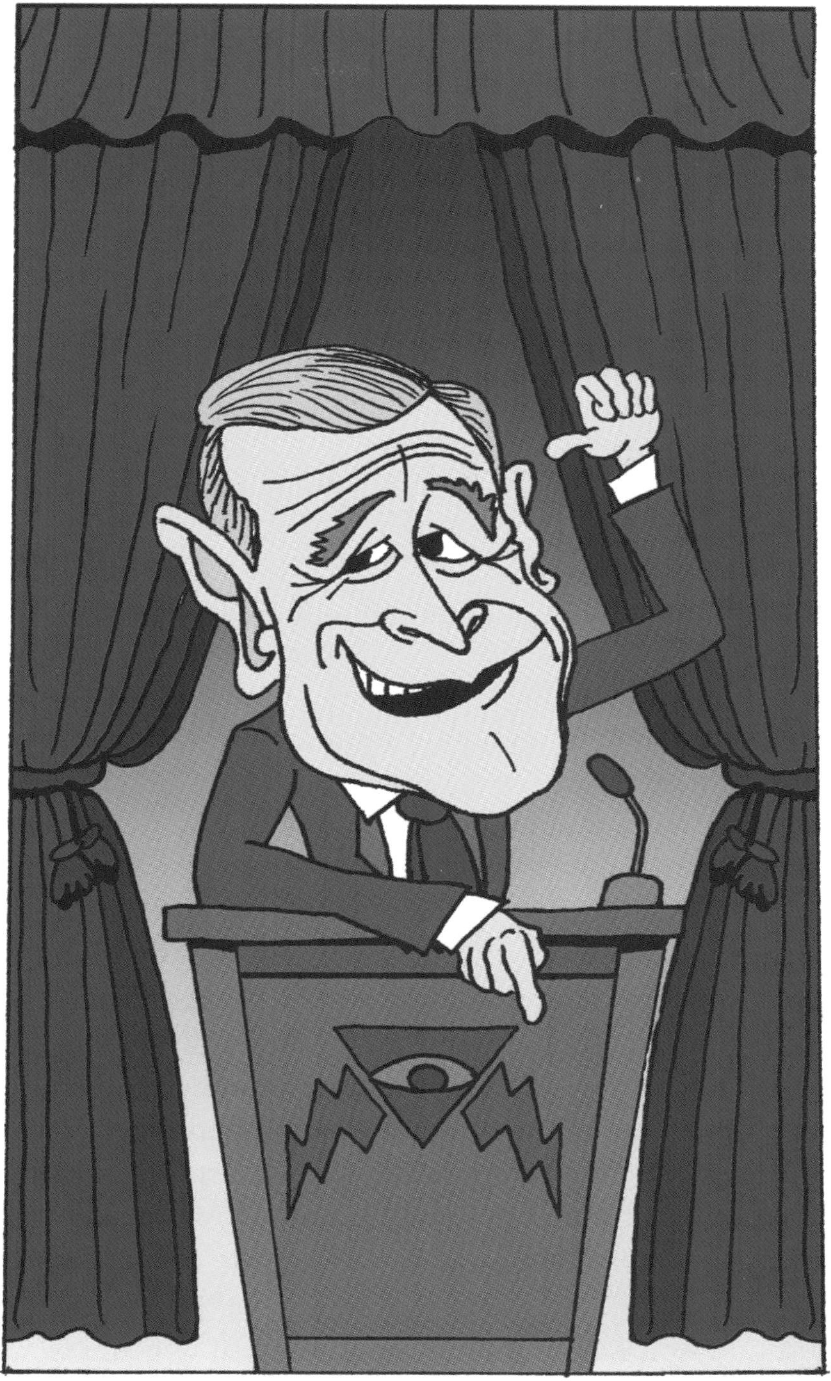

THE BACKSTABBER: This non-confrontational type is also found on both levels and, as their name implies, they do their snaky deeds behind the scenes. BSBSs work at making their 'bitees' feel safe and cozy and then they cruelly betray them. If caught, a plethora of rationale is readily available and will slide off their tongues with ease and eloquence. Many work in sales or marketing positions, and the corporate environment is often a comforting warm rock. All the social niceties will be attended to, and their manners will be impeccable, but be assured they are quite dangerous. Take your time making any decision where a BSBS may be involved. Always read the fine print and if you have any doubt, obtain trustworthy legal counsel. If you're hearing everything you want to hear and everything seems perfect, you're probably listening to a Backstabber.

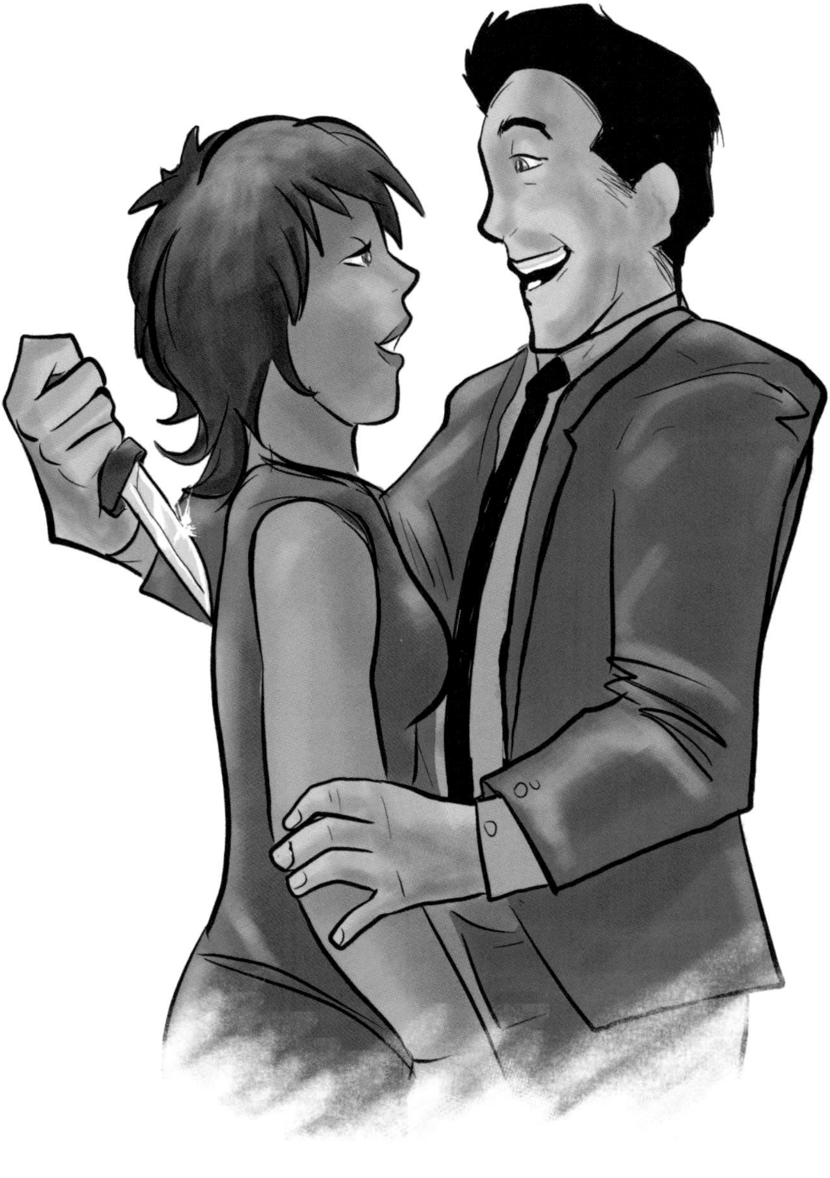

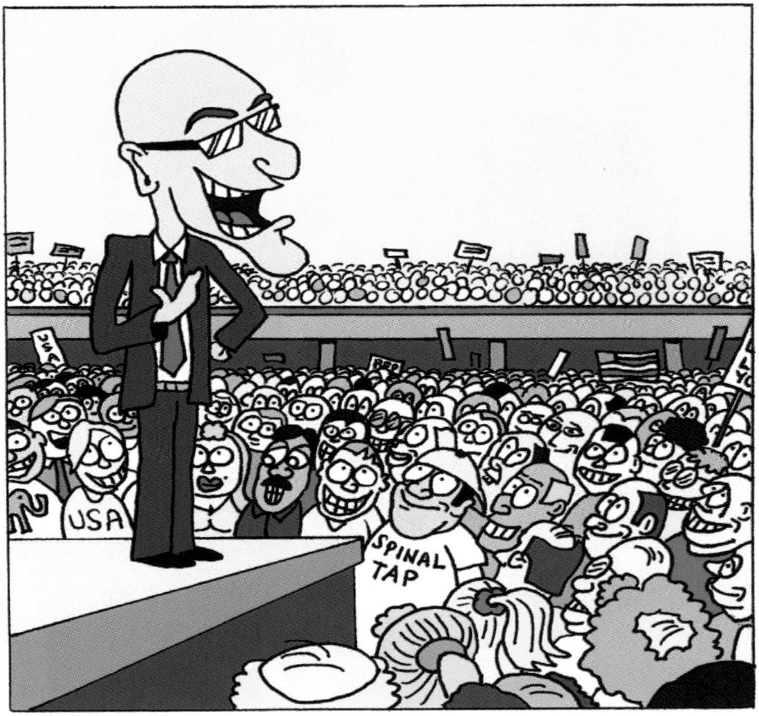
USA
USA
SPINAL TAP

The Bombast Entertainer: A Public Level Two Legged Snake with the gift of gab. Truth or functionality is not important because winning on the field of rhetoric means everything. BS news and talk show hosts are the most obvious examples. There are claims that some are just pure entertainers and that they don't have an agenda, but that's just a lot of BSing. Most knew the mocumentary band Spinal Tap wasn't real, but that didn't stop thousands from believing they were.

The Bilker: This fiduciarily oriented Bipedal Snake is usually found giving financial advice on news or investment shows. The persuasive technique of demanding (covered in the 'techniques' section) is frequently used—at times with a haughty, academic air, and at other times in a big booming voice, full of confidence. Nassim Taleb, in his *New York Times* best-seller *The Black Swan: The Impact of the Highly Improbable*, deftly describes the Bilker: "Based on empirical records, they usually don't know more about profiting in the financial markets than the general population. However, they are much better at narrating about them, or worse, at smoking you with complicated mathematical models."

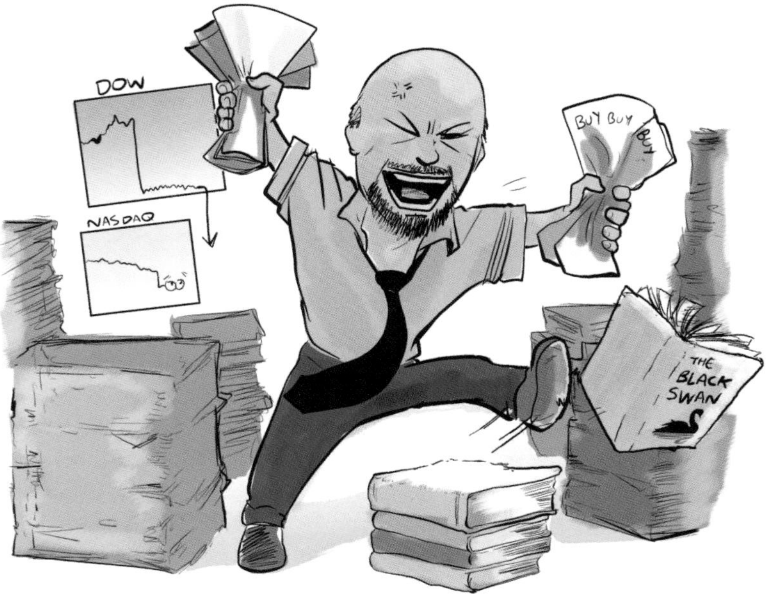
DOW
NASDAQ
BUY BUY
BUY
THE BLACK SWAN

THE DECORATED: This flashy subspecies actively pretends to be scrupulous by displaying trust and 'come hither' cues vociferously. Naive non-snakes can become romantically involved with Decorateds too quickly. This often leads to the 'Las Vegas Wedding, Mexican Divorce' syndrome. Found in both domains, they are usually charming, often attractive, and unilaterally narcissistic. Though typically a bit dim, they are frequently drawn to both leadership roles and tanning salons. Their danger range is moderate to high and romance is a flavored trap. Bigamists, gold diggers, many entertainers, and some politicians populate this colorful category.

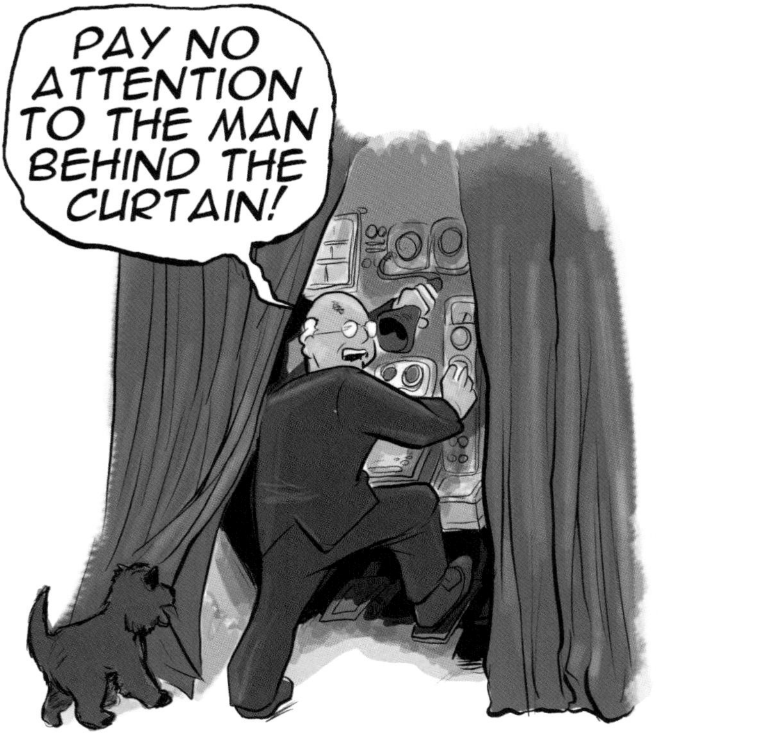
PAY NO ATTENTION TO THE MAN BEHIND THE CURTAIN!

The Misdirector: This type can operate on the D2D level, as a public figure, a behind-the-scenes decision maker, or all of the above. Misdirectors work to keep you focused on the nonessential while de-emphasizing relevant concerns. Fear is commonly used to control their bitees, and flags of negative consequences will be waved at anything that's not supportive of their agenda. Greed, prevalence, and 'getting away with it' are their main concerns. The term 'moral conscience' often brings a chilling sneer. Avoid this dangerously intelligent Two Legged Snake type whenever possible.

THE RHETORICAL: A brawler with words, they lust for victory in the ring of debate. A good one knows every trick in the book: misassociation, misdirection, attack on credentials, using opponents irrelevant imperfections as proof of ineptness, loud talking, outpacing, bringing up irrelevant topics to confuse the issues, taunting, disproportioning, misstatement of facts, citing false experts, outright lying, and the list goes on *(whew!)*. They're aggressive and rarely concede a point. It's a big job to come out on top in an interaction with a Rhetorical, as they are practiced, and winning is irrationally important.

THE SITUATIONAL: This usually D2D type can be hard to see because sometimes they're snaky and sometimes they're not. Many will be nefarious only with some people in their social environment; this is called two-faced or multi-faced snaking.

Some are only BSs in certain areas, such as romance or finance. Stress can be a huge 'on switch', as can alcohol and/or drugs. Their risk range is wide: While most are merely annoying, others are quite dangerous.

The Media Maven: A Public Level Bipedal Snake, their motivation is to sell more media and pedal more influence through the use of amplified hype and over-dramatization. All types of snaky techniques come into play with MMBSs, but the #1 tactic is using fear. They'll play up the danger of a story so people will tune in, again and again and again to make sure they're doing all they can to prevent becoming victim to the next weather disaster, plague of disease, or toaster recall. This type often works in close collusion with political BSs, so their news feeds will be fast and unrestricted.

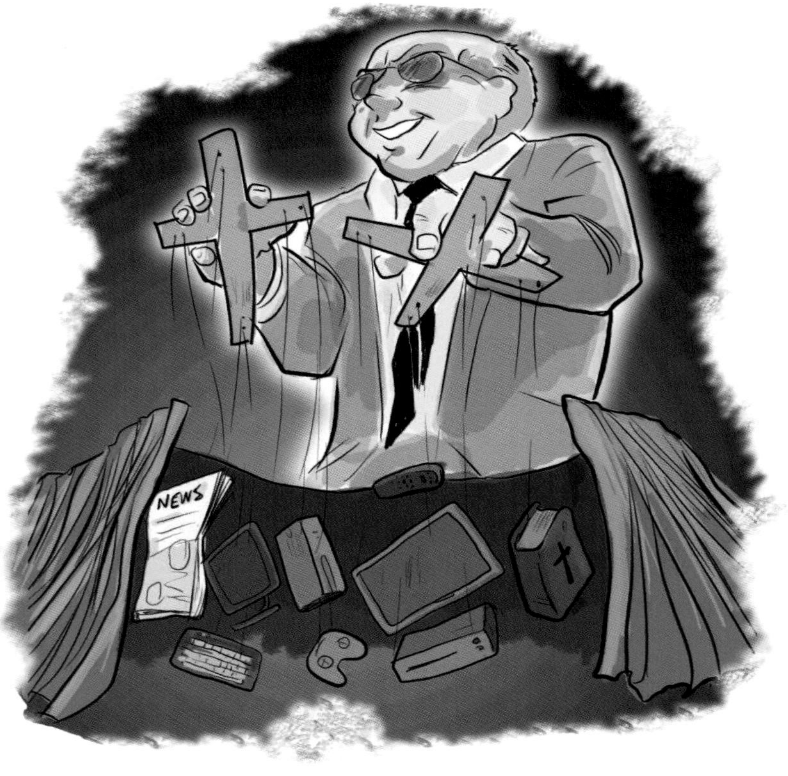
NEWS

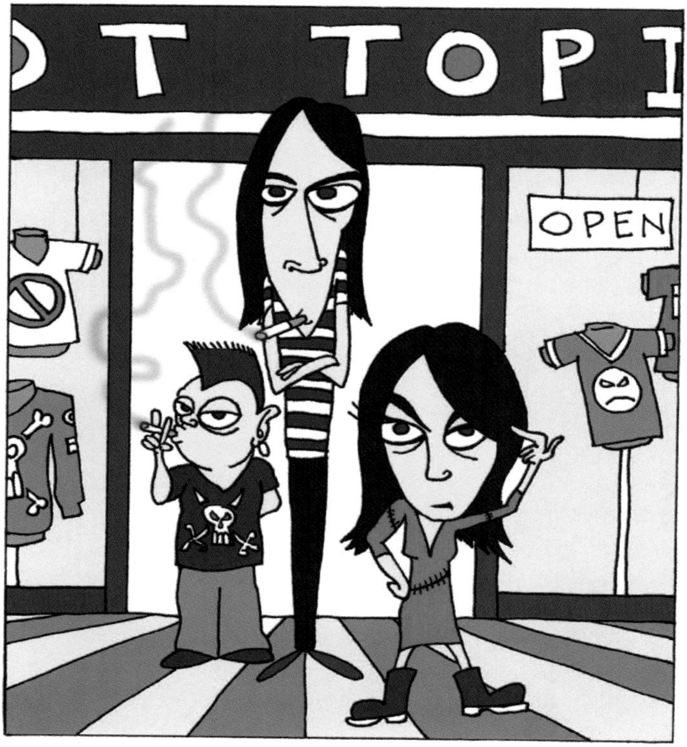
T TOP
OPEN

The Lost: This usually D2D model is emotionally immature and has low self-esteem. Many act as if filled with world weary anger and say "whatever" a lot. Others are big talkers who use unnecessarily complex and obvious mental gymnastics in attempts to dupe their bitee. They're dishonest with themselves and others and are overly sympathetic to other BSs. A few try not to be snaky, but poor impulse control makes that hard. Drug and alcohol problems are common. LBSs are often found in retail shopping malls, loitering in and around trendy stores.

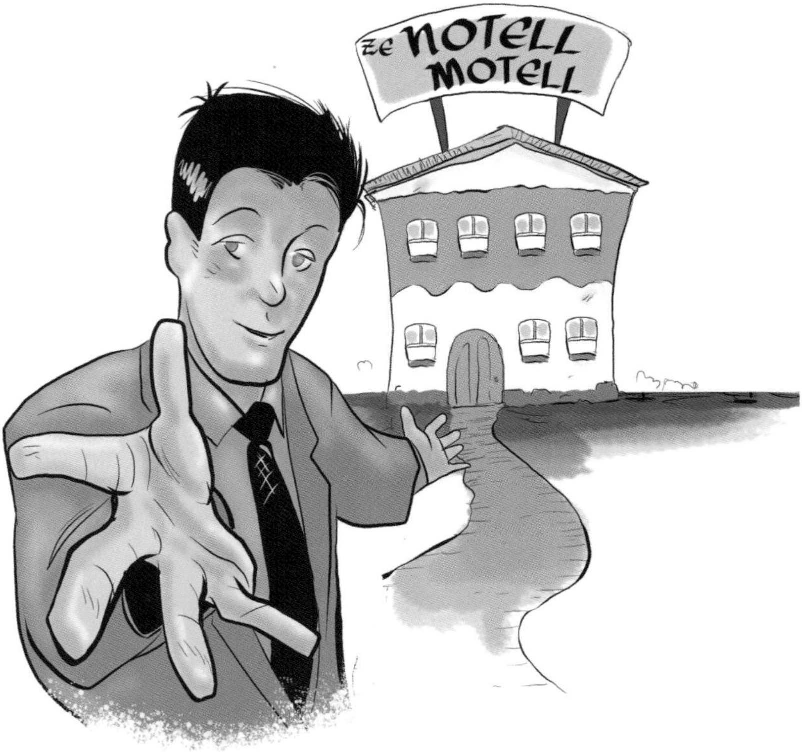
ZE NOTELL
MOTELL

The Lifer: Found on both levels, Lifers come off as slick and super confident. They usually smell really good too. Money and relationship problems abound in their personal lives, but their hair and clothes are always perfect. Get rich quick deals, shaky real estate investments, and ponzi schemes are classic Lifer bites. Lifers are very prone to inappropriate sexual liaisons so moderately priced motels attract large numbers of this acquisition-oriented BS on any given weekday afternoon. Their risk range is wide, from nearly transcendent to sleazy and exploitive. Though usually easy to spot, don't leave your wallet out.

The Justified: Rather the opposite of the Backstabber, this subspecies is confrontational and is usually found at D2D levels. Justifieds feel they are entitled to their snaky behavior because they see virtually all people as BSs or suckers, unenlightened to the world's true nature. Mobsters, thugs, and criminals of all types populate this category. Lower level JBSs are known to look for romance in the personal ads of local weekly papers, frequently while incarcerated. The implication is that they're softhearted types who've been badly hurt, have adopted a tough persona to compensate, and need love and understanding to change. A small percentage of this snake type probably is sincere, but proceed with extreme caution. Many use this sympathetic dynamic at great consequence to those on the receiving end of their attentions.

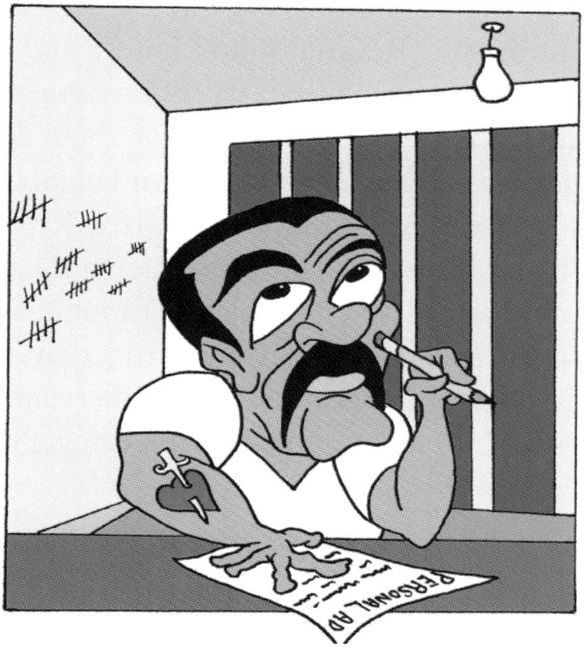
PERSONAL AD

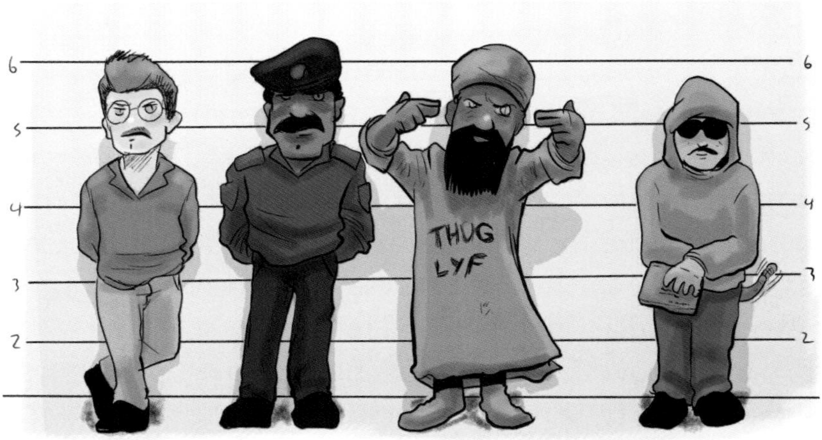
THUG
LYF

The King Cobra: King Cobras don't see themselves as Bipedal Snakes, but they are, and wildly so. A high political or religious office is commonly used as a front. Joseph Stalin, the Reverend Jim Jones, and Saddam Hussein are examples of this nasty BS. Passionate oratory and feigned nobility attempt to cover their delusional and dangerous nature. Often racists and bigots, they are cruel and persecutional. Subconsciously, King Cobras want to be loved, and then they hate those who love them. Some of the less intelligent, though still quite vicious, D2D specimens can be found driving older, poorly maintained panel vans. Serial killers, murderers, and genocidal lunatics populate this category. Stay as far away as possible. *(Duh!)*.

THE TRANSCENDENTS: These people were Bipedal Snakes, but they've grown past the BS value system and understand its selfish and destructive nature. Transcendents have learned from their time on the dark side and they do not share the motivations and goals of Bipedal Snakes. Trustworthy and loving, many are excellent teachers and leaders who enjoy using their wealth of experience to make positive contributions.

Now that you have a basic understanding of types, it's time to go snake watching. Many will not be found in their pure form but in amalgamations of different types and intensities. Frequently, camouflage is used by more aware TLSs; good deeds, dressing to blend in with the social environment, projecting a sweet demeanor, associations with charitable organizations, etc., etc. This makes it a good idea to take as much time as possible to decide if you are observing a BS or not.

Effective snake identification takes practice and is a skill set that can always be improved upon. Refer back to these chapters until your snake spotting becomes a habit. *It's more fun to snake watch than be snake bit.*

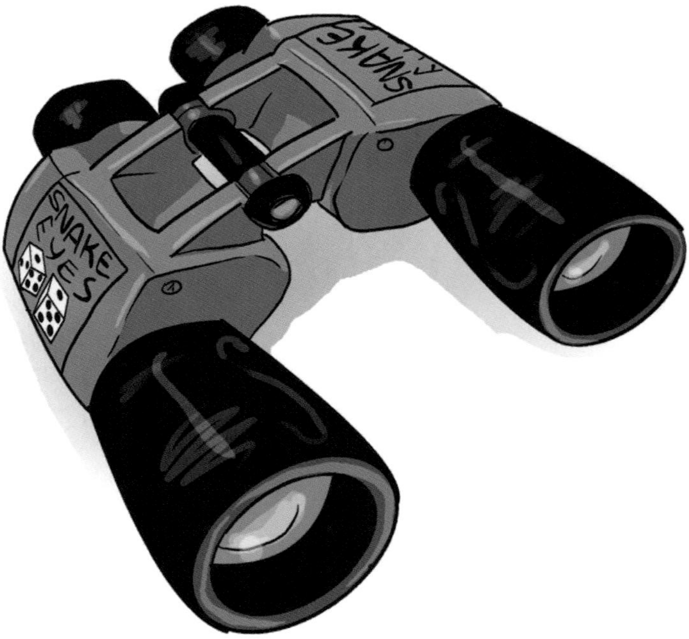
SNAKE
SNAKE EYES

The Apple Biters: Types of Two Legged Snake Fans

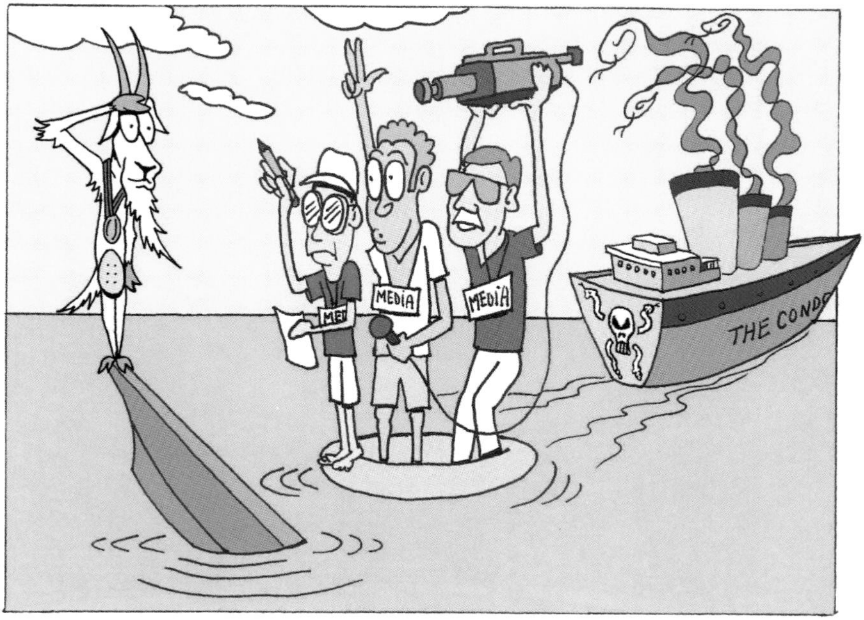
MEDIA
MEDIA
THE CONDO

Public Bipedal Snakes need Apple Biters like rock stars need fans: Without them they're just not a big deal. Being an Apple Biter fulfills the BS fans' desire to feel needed, safe, powerful, and important. Their uses range from being cash providers and voters to public speaking, administrative work, recruiting new biters and, on occasion, being a sacrificial scapegoat for the cause.

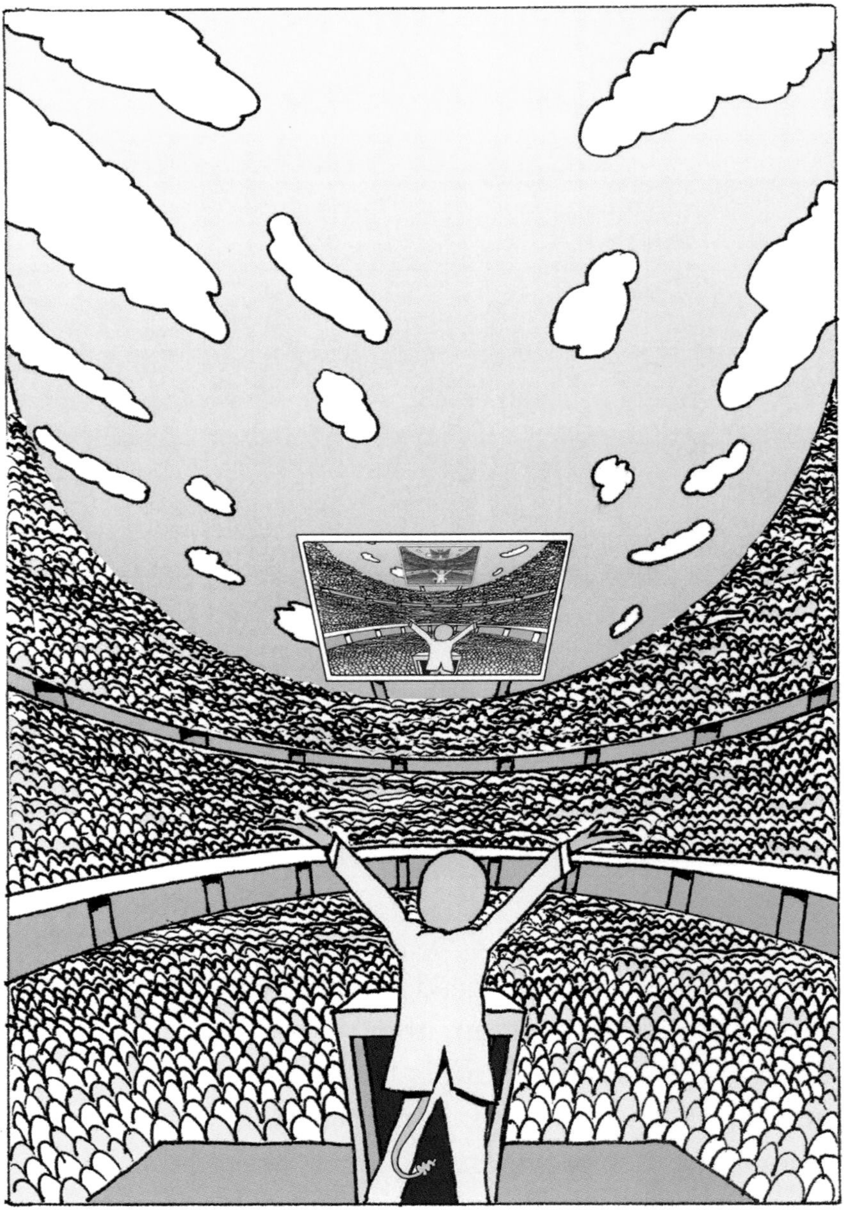

The more fans a BS has, the more power he holds.

Recognizing Apple Biters is just as important as being aware of TLSs, perhaps more so. BS fans are often on the lookout for new recruits and frequently get aggressive on behalf of the TLSs they follow. The passion they have for their cause can make them convincing and quite dangerous.

THE TRUE BELIEVER: Blinded by need, passion, and symbolic rhetoric, these fans don't have the ability to identify even outrageous BSing. TBBSFs are particularly vulnerable because of their hunger for social acceptance. They didn't get picked for sports teams when in school, relationships haven't gone well, and work just isn't satisfying. They've never really felt they fit in. Bipedal Snakes who tell them they are important, appreciated, and right in their opinions will be resolutely followed. They make highly effective public speakers because they truly believe in the agenda they support. Many become Two Legged Snakes themselves.

The WannaBe: This type of fan has loads of emotional baggage and compensates for it by following Bipedal Snakes that have the same sort of baggage. WBBSFs relate to their chosen BS as a projected version of themselves and then put them on a pedestal. They frequently find ways to actively support their BS and will work long hours without complaint. Loud, emotional, call-and-response bombast at the rallies of political and religious Bipedal Snakes provides these Apple Biters with much needed emotional release.

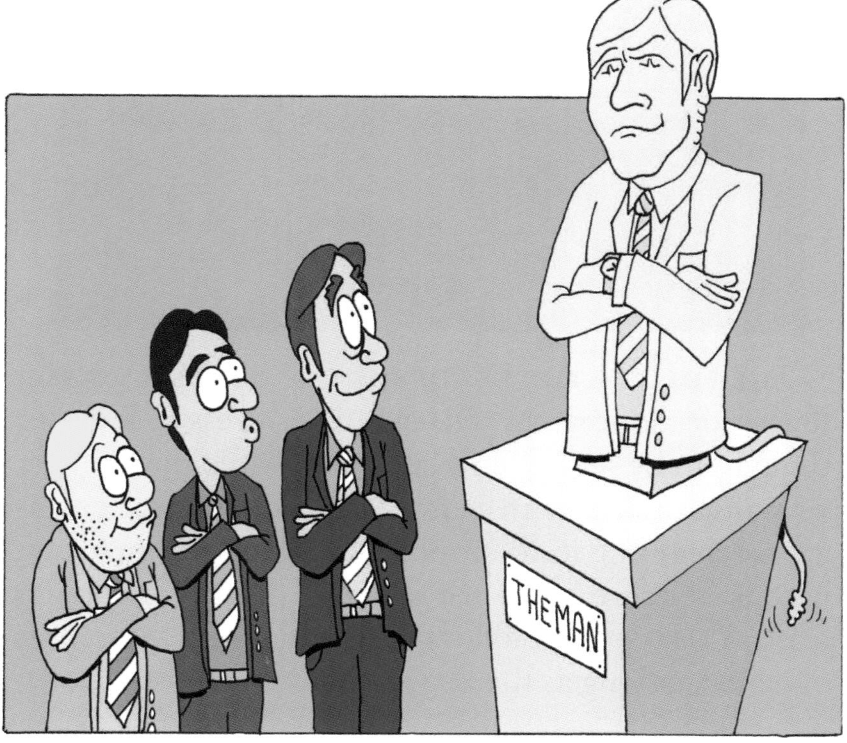
THEMAN

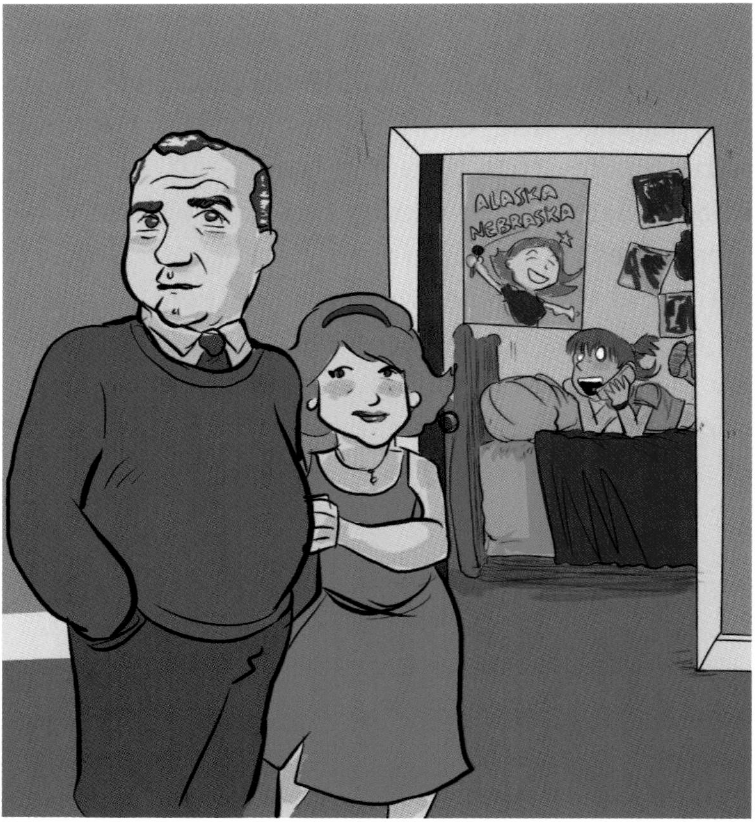
ALASKA
NEBRASKA

The Follow the Leader: This is a fan subservient to the social hierarchy. Older FLBSFs dress in fashions thought to be severe ten years prior, while the younger versions are akin to an army of pierced, starstruck teenagers screaming for their pop star. They feel important because they are associated with the winning or popular team. This type will follow their leader into the depths of denial, as long as their special status holds out.

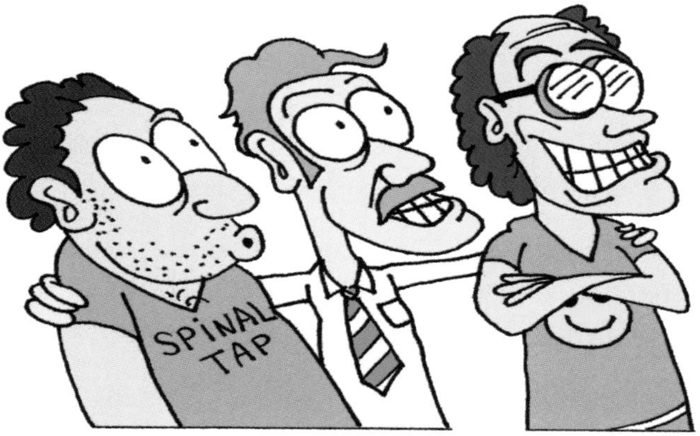
SPINAL
TAP

The Loyalists: By far the largest fan category, they number in the millions. Most were brought up in households that maintain a sentimental, anti-change perspective, and they remain loyal to that belief system, no matter what. LBSFs are often put on display as examples of the innocent, truthful, down-home, regular folks the Two Legged Snake's cause supposedly supports, but in reality cruelly misuses. This fan type is unquestioningly loyal, often kindhearted, and almost always votes.

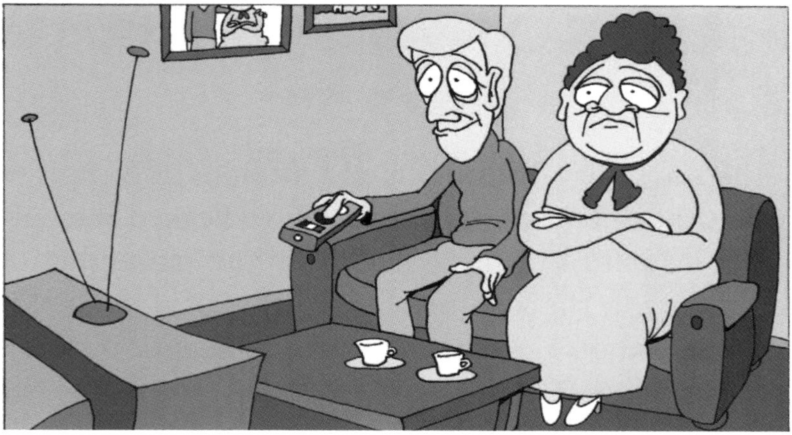

It's a huge expenditure of time, at best, to try to reason with an Apple Biter, as virtually all are steadfast in their support of the BS cause they believe in. At rallies they can get themselves worked up into such a state of righteousness that violence erupts. Making it a habit to recognize BS fans, so you can see them coming and avoid their games, is time well spent indeed.

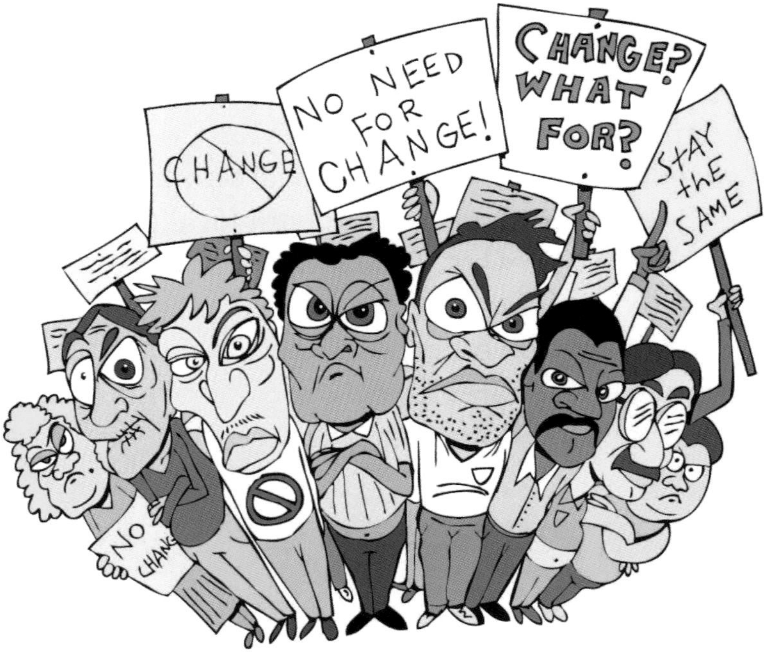
CHANGE
NO NEED FOR CHANGE!
CHANGE? WHAT FOR?
STAY the SAME
NO CHANG

There are literally millions and millions of BS fans who follow the dogma of their chosen Two Legged Snakes. At times it's hard to tell the fans from the snakes but they are different; the fans need to be part of a group while the BSs do not. However that doesn't make Apple Biters any less dangerous.

> **"** Fool me once, shame on you.
> Fool me twice, shame on me. **"**

Common Two Legged Snake Persuasive Techniques

Debate and persuasive techniques, when practiced with good intentions are useful tools that help us find the best solutions to problems and the wisest paths to follow. When used by Two Legged Snakes these techniques are powerful weapons for persuading people to act against their own best interests and 'win'! for the BS cause, usually at ridiculous costs. Awareness is essential because if you're not aware, you can easily be subject to snaky persuasive power.

To begin spotting snaky plays, ask yourself:

- Does the pitch seem logical or does it emphasize charisma, symbolic association, or wordplay? President Clinton's legalistic dissection of what constitutes sex during his impeachment trial comes to mind as an example of speaking with a forked tongue.
- Does the pitch feel truthful and motivated by contribution or does it seem overly animated and gestural? An eye rolling, sneering, posturing debate opponent is certainly motivated to win but how truthful do you think they are?
- Are you asked to believe something, give something, or buy something? Does the intensity level seem disproportionately high, and seeking appeal from emotion?

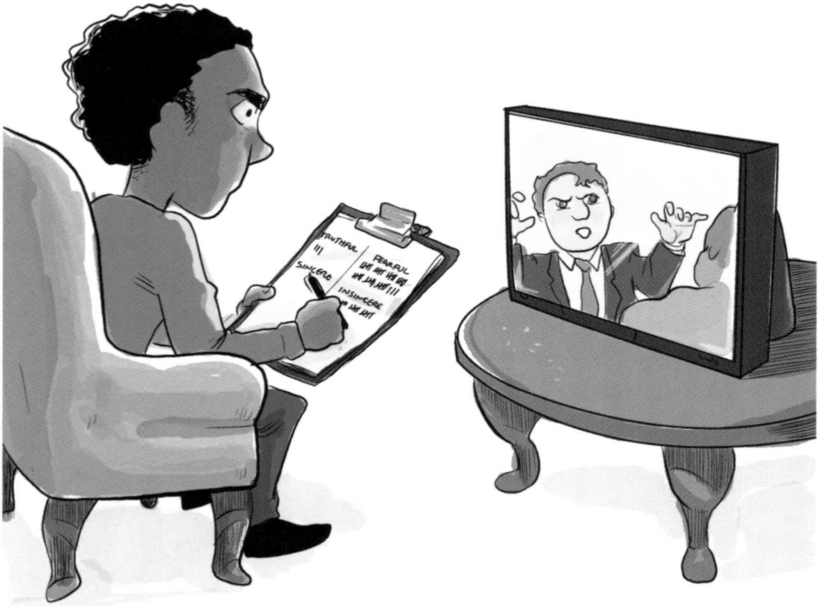
TRUTHFUL
SINCERE
FEARFUL
INSINCERE

The vast majority of us struggle to balance our self-aware, rational mind with our more impulsive, instinctual natures. This is no easy task and to complicate matters BSs frequently try to use this quandary to their advantage.

In their best-selling book *How to Spot a Liar*, Hartly and Karinch point out that appeals to emotion tend to access primitive parts of our brains that are reactive and animalistic. The higher brain stem locations that are more suited for analysis are then largely bypassed. BSs tailor many of their orations and pitches to this phenomenon. Passionate speaking often includes a good dose of emotion, but it's not the over-stimulation of BS rhetoric. Watch out for attempts to exploit your reactive animalistic side. Stay rational and snaky persuasion will have much less pull.

The following is a list of some of the everyday techniques BSs use. They come up with new gambits all the time, so the list is always growing. But no matter how sophisticated the pitch, if examined honestly and openly, most have a falseness that's easy to see.

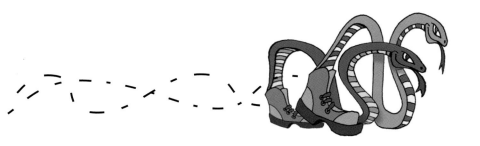

ACCUSINATION: A direct finger-pointing attack that attempts to put the BS's target on the defensive. Most of these attacks are designed not only to harm or discredit the target, but to hide the fact that the BSs do that which they accuse the target of doing. This preemptive strategy can be difficult to respond to. It's important not to get sucked into a childish "no, you did" debate. If you honestly examine what the accusers are saying, it is often laughably ridiculous. BS fans often use this technique to get other Apple Biters whipped up into a frenzy. Some incidents of Accusination are so illogical, they could be termed mass hysteria as I'm sure the tens of thousands of women who were burned at the stake as witches in post reformation Europe would agree. This practice continues to this day in several areas in Africa.

Misdirection: Encouraging a focus on less relevant material to minimize focus on snaky activities. For example, a newscast that spends more time and energy on a local man's fight against graffiti than it gives to the story of a powerful politician being caught lying about significant issues is directing the audience's attention to the less important story. D2D examples include unwarranted changes of topic in order to avoid problem areas.

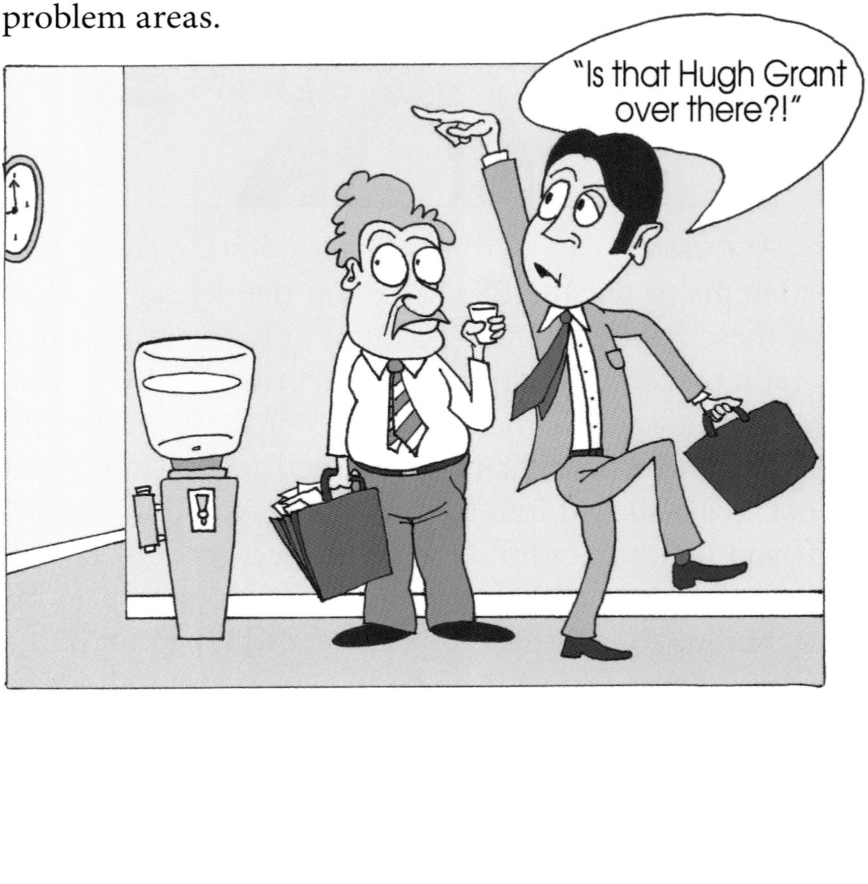
"Is that Hugh Grant over there?!"

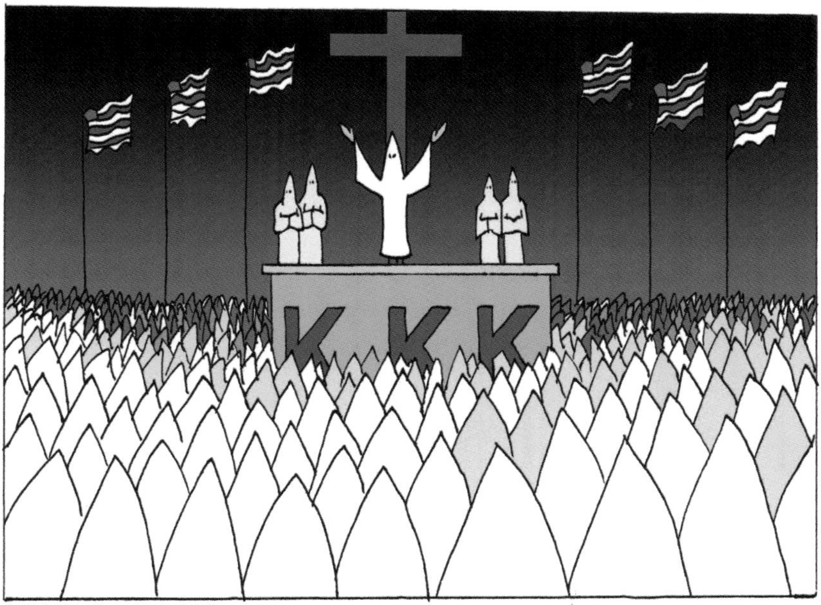
KKK

MISASSOCIATION: Stating or implying that an association exists without proof. This technique comes in both verbal and symbolic forms. American flags on the stage at a Ku Klux Klan rally symbolically misassociates American and Klan values. The statement, "like Abraham Lincoln before me, history will judge my actions," verbally misassociates the speaker's actions, inaccurately implying he is on the same level as the great president.

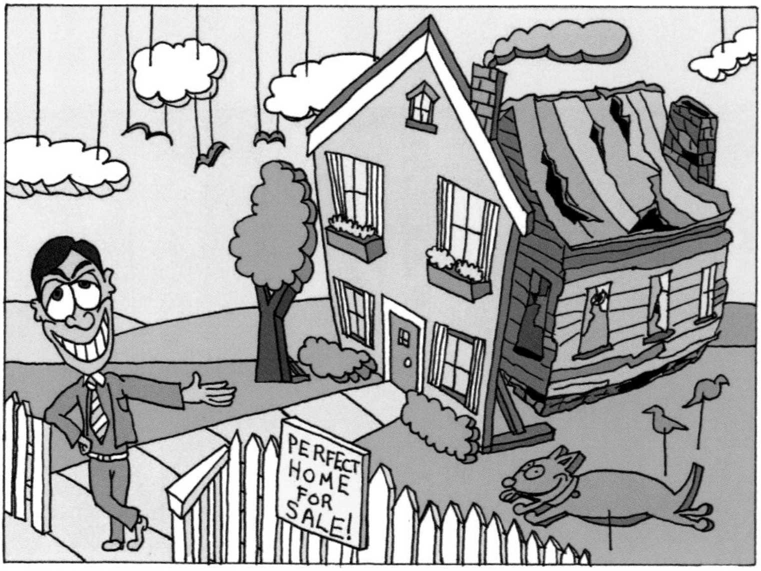
PERFECT
HOME
FOR
SALE!

Going Big: Using any persuasive technique (lying, misdirecting, etc.) to such a huge degree that potential bitees are encouraged to buy the pitch, simply because it seems preposterous that anyone would lie so wildly. For example, "This is one safe and solid house. It was the personal residence of an award-winning contractor. I probably shouldn't tell you this, but the only reason it's priced so low is because he's getting divorced and wants out of it fast." Many fall into this trap, believing it's rude to ask for substantiation. In this example, thoroughly examining the property, checking the contractors resume and status with the licensing board, and getting a home inspection by a respected professional would be the way to go. Trusting what you see rather than believing what you're told easily immunizes you against this technique.

DISPROPORTIONING: Representing the relative variables in a scenario as having a great degree more or less importance than they actually have. Eloquent BSs can make even huge imbalances seem reasonable: "While it's true that my client misappropriated a significant amount of money (billions of US dollars) from his clients, it is important to remember that he is 70 years old. This late in his life, the rigors of a regular prison would be too much and would amount to a cruel and unusual punishment. House arrest is the appropriate choice for a man of his infirmity, who has no history of violence and is not a threat to anyone."

RAVE-UP QUESTIONING: This technique utilizes a series of questions to amplify a pitch by encouraging the audience's emotional response. The questions are asked repeatedly, with an increasing volume that ends in an emotional crescendo: "My friends are we here tonight, under this glorious tent, in support of the holy bombast? Yes! Are we here to spread the bombast gospel that we know is the only true word of God? Yes! Then let us give generously to the collection plate and take to the streets with handmade signs that herald our slogans of truth and wisdom, so we may picket the heathens and guide them with our wise judge-mentality". Through the emotional bond they feel with the other fans, this team-building and opinion-directing technique strengthens the fans' belief in the BS agenda.

Burlesquing: Reducing a subject or point of view to a distinct set of features that are then distorted and exaggerated to support a pitch or discredit a non-BS agenda: "Jeez Laura, you can't believe a word that skank says. She spends all her time making sure her boobs look perky and her lipstick's on right. She smells like she fell into the 'super hooch' perfume tank. No way did she see me with Juanita last night".

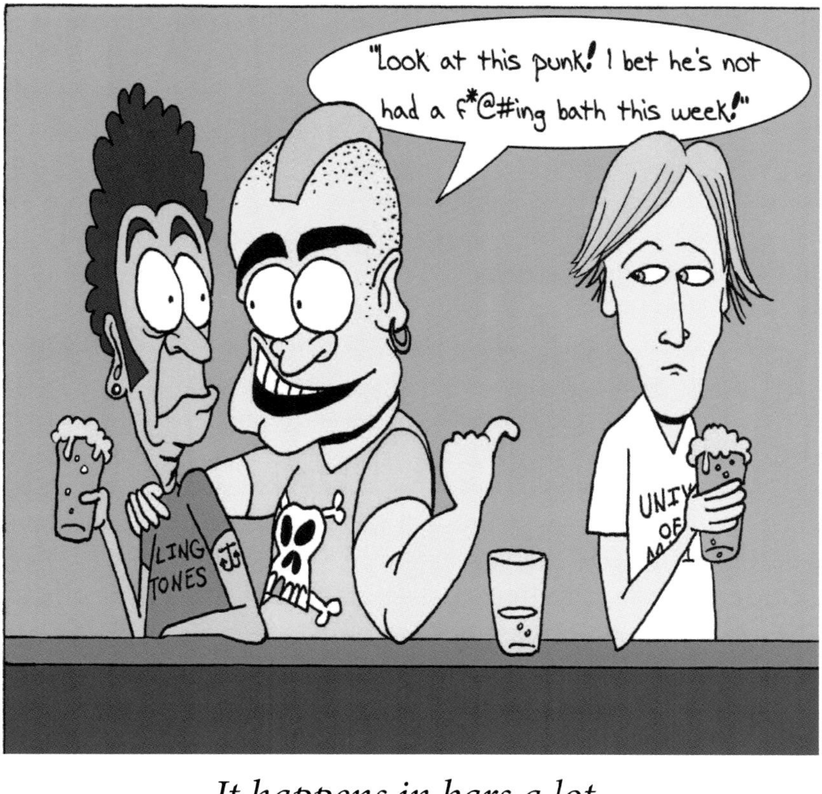
"Look at this punk! I bet he's not had a f*@#ing bath this week!"
LING TONES
JJ
UNIV OF

It happens in bars a lot.

BOMBASTING: Using loud and emotional speech. This 'louder is more righteous' association is used liberally at Bipedal Snakes' meetings and rallies. It gets the crowds pumped up and feeling powerful. On the D2D level, this behavior indicates severe control issues and is often accompanied by an unpleasant musky aroma.

VIPERATION: Vicious name-calling. Bipedal Snake talk show hosts do this a lot. Religious BSs get into it too, but they don't use profanity, just 'hell this' and 'Satan that' references. Viperation is an excellent snake spotter as non-BSs only do this under extreme stress, particularly in professional situations. If you observe this on the D2D level, run!

Overtalking: Not letting anyone get a word in edgewise. Cutting off opposing viewpoints and basically interrupting any dissenting opinions. How rude.

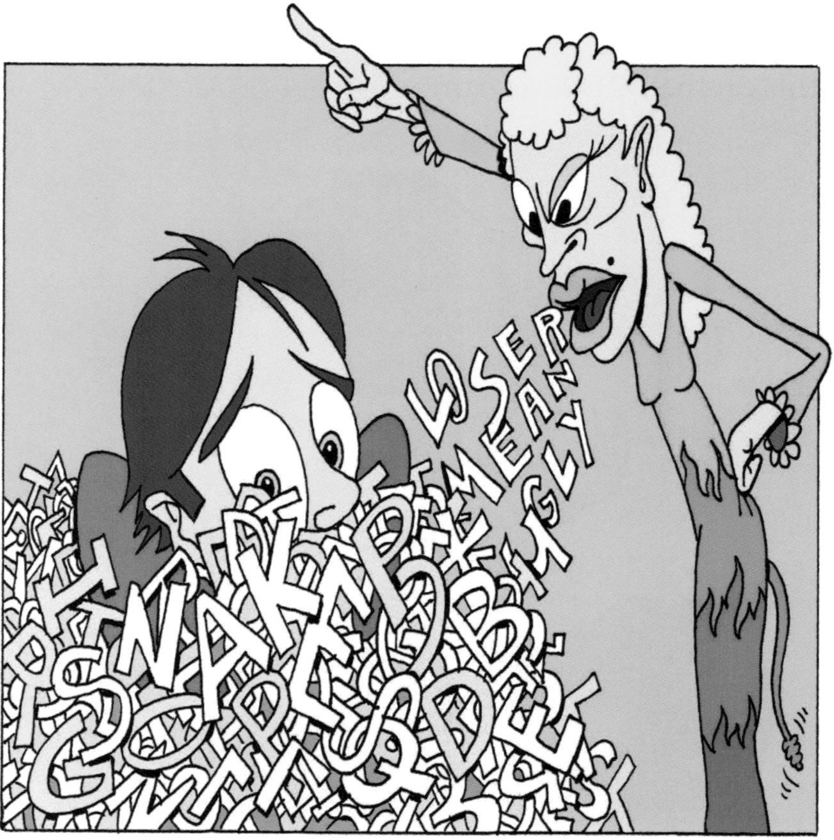
LOSER
MEAN
UGLY

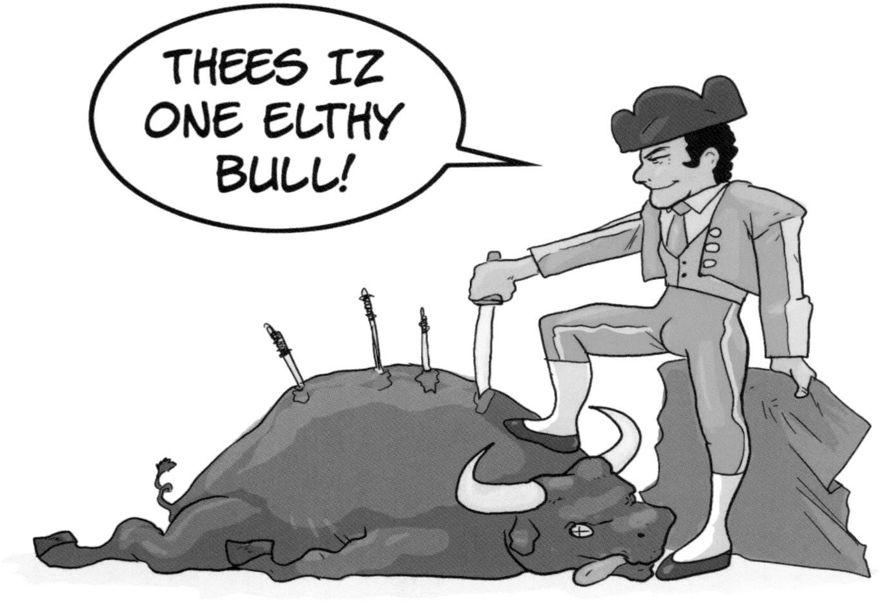
THEES IZ ONE ELTHY BULL!

Demanding: Telling people what they must or mustn't do, or making a statement that asserts absolute knowledge in a situation where that's not possible. This is often seen in the realm of economic forecasting: "I'm telling you to buy stock in Deer Stones Funds right now (an investment banking firm that will shut its doors for good in two days). This is a strong, undervalued company and I know it will be trading at over $80 per share within two months."

BEGGING SYMPATHY: A Two Legged Snake in retreat appeal to emotion. The river of tears the Reverend Jim Baker cried when he was caught bilking his faithful TV audience is a great Public Level example. This technique comes in many syrupy flavors, and in most cases is easily differentiated from sincere sorrow by its switch-like 'on and off' nature and smarmy presentation. D2D relationship versions can be seen on several confrontation oriented weekday afternoon TV programs that present security guard buffeted relationship betrayals before a large studio audience.

Flattery: A Bipedal Snake pitch initiator. To soften up a potential bitee, complements, admiration, and even fandom are used to create the right atmosphere. An unquestioningly trusting, scrutiny free, and buzzed on ego bitee is an easy sell.

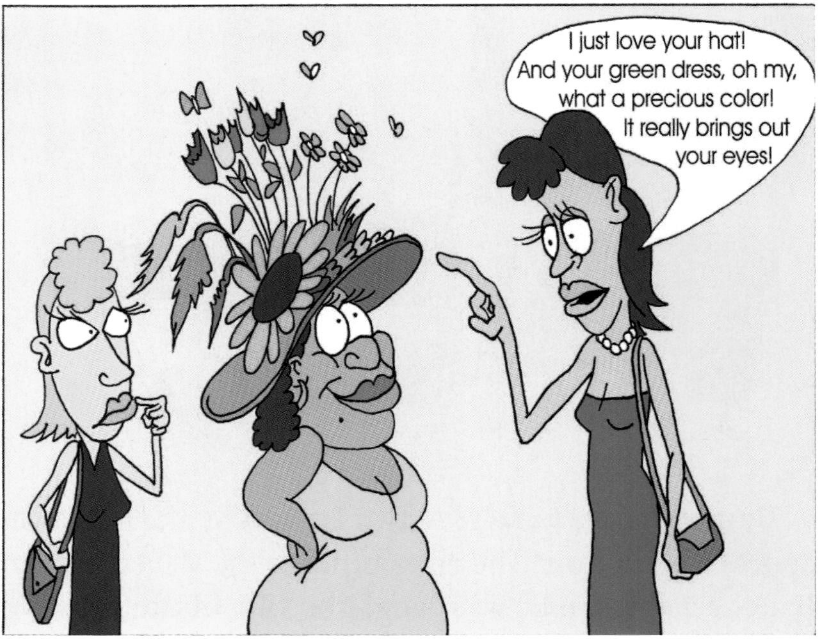
I just love your hat!
And your green dress, oh my,
what a precious color!
It really brings out
your eyes!

"Have you lost weight? I love what you've done with the place! Wherever did you get that glorious hat?" and "Omigosh, I've been a fan of your work forever" are corny examples of ploys to get potential bitee's defenses down and their trust up. It's surprising how often this technique works.

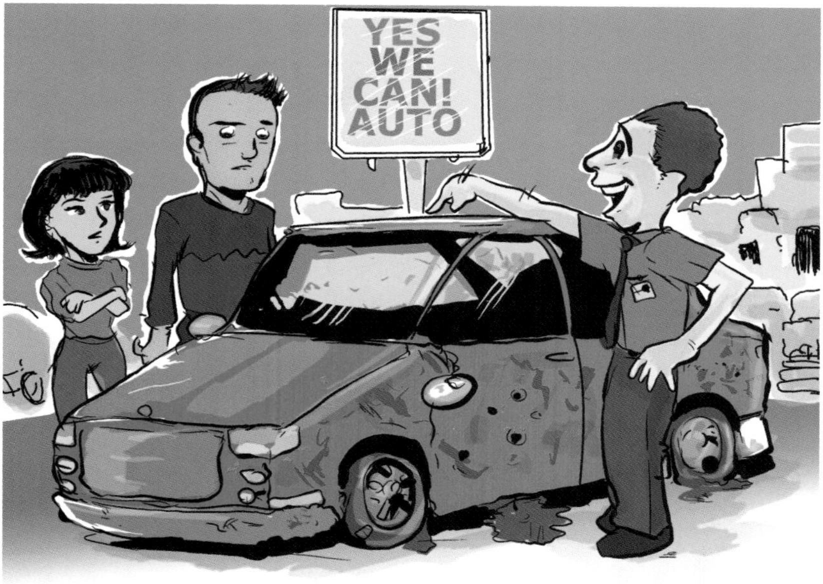
YES
WE
CAN!
AUTO

Yes Setting: Asking a series of questions that have a uniformly 'yes' (or 'no') answer, the last of which supports the pitch. This is a technique that has been used for years, in a variety of contexts: "Is it important that we keep our children safe? Should we protect them from dangers within our school systems? Are you voting 'yes' on prop 24 so our kids are safe from the threat of homosexual teachers?"

D2D salespeople use this one too: "Do you want a great value-to-dollar ratio? Are you looking for a car that has an excellent safety record? Do you want a complete warranty package included in the price? If I can show you a model with all of these features and excellent financing, are you ready to drive your new car home today?"

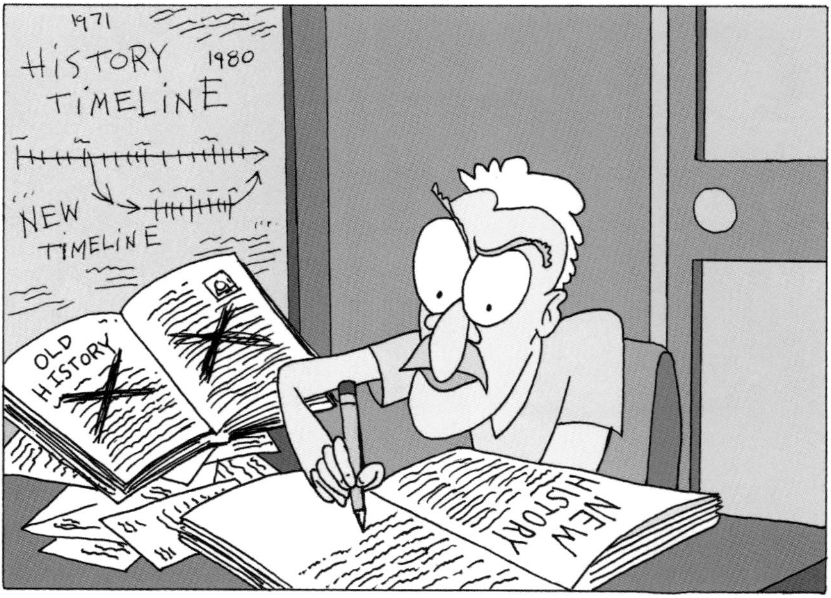
1971
HISTORY 1980
TIMELINE
NEW
TIMELINE
OLD
HISTORY
NEW
HISTORY

Reinventing History: This technique is popular and often works because well-intended, problem solving people tend to deal with the issues of the day and move on. If a BS feels what really happened may be forgotten or the details are perhaps blurry, he will often reinvent what occurred and attempt to win a battle he's already lost. If successful, this new history is used as traction to further his present goals.

Now that you're familiar with common snaky ploys, make it a tradition to spot them as often as you can. New ones come up all the time so when you spot a fresh snaky manipulation give it a name, a description, and post it on www.twoleggedsnakes.com. Include a picture if you like. The more we know the less likely we are to feel the fangs.

Two Legged Snake Biting Styles

It is important to note that Two Legged Snakes approach biting with varying styles and intensities. Public level BSs rely on sophistry and charisma and instruct their bitees as to what to believe and what to do. D2D BSs are much more physical in their attacks. Being aware of their styles can help you remove yourself from the critical path forewarned (as if you'd heard the rattle of a rattlesnake). The following lists the three main biting styles used by D2D Bipedal Snakes.

THE NIBBLER: This slinky style hides in the shadows and often uses small 'test bites' to see what can be gotten away with. If they get caught what they did isn't usually that bad (at first), so their consequences are minimal. Nibblers are timid and prefer smaller game so they're risk level is less. Office managers who consistently pilfer tiny amounts of money (that end up being huge sums) from the companies they work for are a frequently seen example. Keeping an eye on the small stuff is the only way to protect yourself from this sneaky biting style.

Child molesters are also frequently nibblers. They use 'grooming bites' to work their way into a position of trust, progressively gaining the child's confidence by being kind and positive and becoming more physical with them only in small increments. When a certain level of trust is reached the inappropriate sexual activity ensues. The nibbler then confuses the child by pretending the molestation was what the child wanted or controls them with threats, so their snaky deeds stay hidden. The threats often include violence to the child's loved ones, including pets. Although molesting nibblers are very dangerous, since they operate 'in the dark' you can keep your children safe by simply being aware of their whereabouts and counseling them firmly not to allow themselves to be alone with strangers and to report any touching activity immediately, even if it's a person the child knows well.

THE CHOMPER: This Biting style is used by snaky salespeople. Time constraint ("available at this price today only"), badgering argument, and group pressure is used to position a bitee to buy, buy, buy! Term life insurance, major household appliances, and vacation time share condominiums are products that seem exclusively the domain of this biting style. Some chomper building contractors use the 'bait and switch' technique of promising something they never intend to provide ("we'll have that roof on by next week") to get their bitees to sign on the dotted line and then switch to doing whatever's best for them ("as your contract stipulates we can choose to change the estimated completion date at our discretion. We should be able to get your roof done in six months, barring any unforeseen…") Chomp! Always read the fine print.

THE POUNCER: This patient bite style entails waiting until the time is right and then making the snaky move. Often a series of conditioning bites is used to get the bitee in the right place for the big bite. For example, let's say snaky Renee covets her friend Laura's boyfriend, Luke. Renee's a pouncer so she makes it her business to get alone with Luke as much as possible. When they are alone she sees what she can get away with using innuendo about how she'd love to find a man like Luke and how she admires him and on and on. Of course, that's accompanied by a plethora of positioning bites like touching him lightly, long 'eye to eye' moments, and plenty of negative comments about Laura. When unwitting and naive Luke has been properly conditioned, Renee pounces and she and Luke are in Belize when Laura gets the breakup letter. Pouncers usually prey on the not so bright and are shamelessly artful at being two-faced. Many Charmers, Lifers, and Situationals use this biting style to achieve their snaky goals.

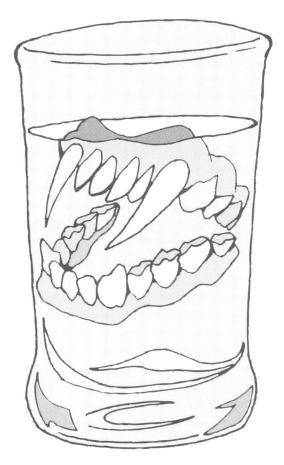

Remember to keep your eyes open for the 'set up' of these biting styles. If you feel some nibbles, a load of pressure or too many compliments watch out, a bite may be coming your way!

> " Insanity is doing the same thing over and over again and expecting different results.
> –Albert Einstein "

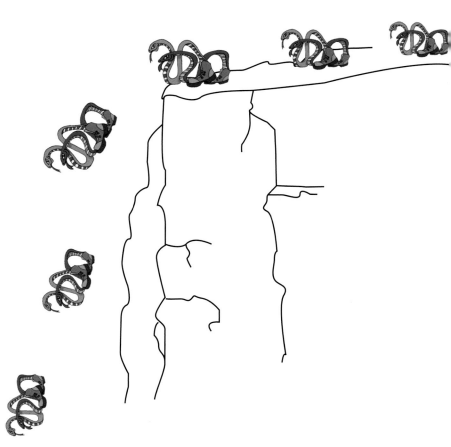

Handling
Two Legged Snakes

Who we listen to greatly affects our levels of happiness and success. Awareness gives us the freedom to make our own decisions, clear of Bipedal Snake rhetoric, so *take the time* to make sure you know who you're dealing with. Don't be pressured into making any choice before you're ready. And *don't hesitate to run.*

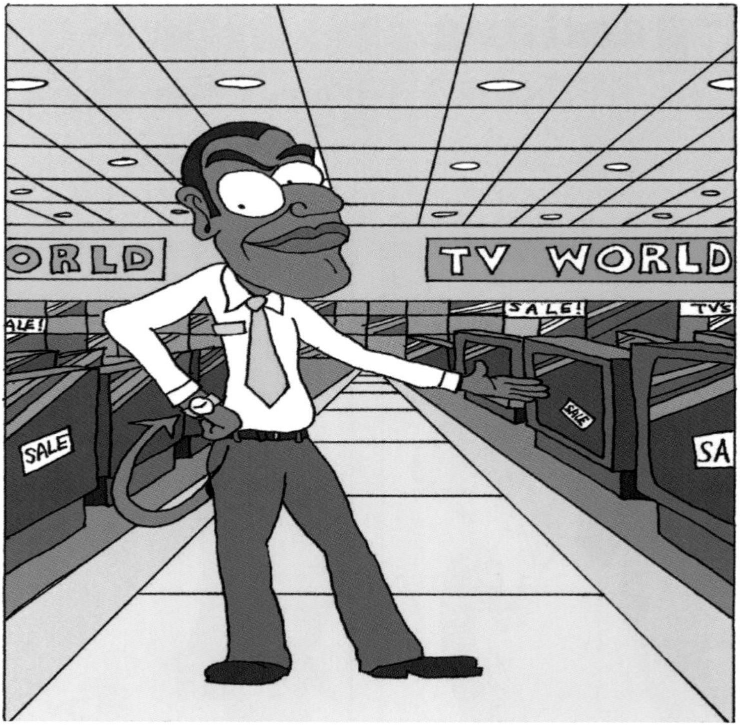
ORLD
TV WORLD
SALE!
TV'S
ALE!
SALE
SALE
SA

Keep your eyes open for 'tells', which are behaviors or inconsistencies that point to a potentially snaky status. For example, many BSs want to move quickly with personal or business decisions. The more time there is to evaluate a pitch, the more likely the snaky elements will be uncovered. If you try to put the decision off and the 'possible' puts pressure on you to choose quickly, a snaky tell is revealed.

Inconsistencies between what a possible BS says and what he actually does is another tell area. In the D2D range, if a possible rarely shows up on time, doesn't return calls, or talks about his charitable acts while you get stuck paying for lunch, it's more than likely you're dealing with a BS. On the public level, unkept promises, a history of telling lies or half-truths, and behavior inconsistent with public image all point sharply to BS status.

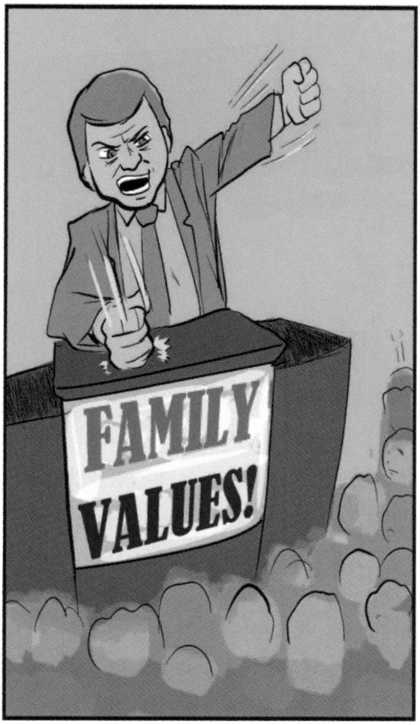
FAMILY
VALUES!

July 12th, 11AM

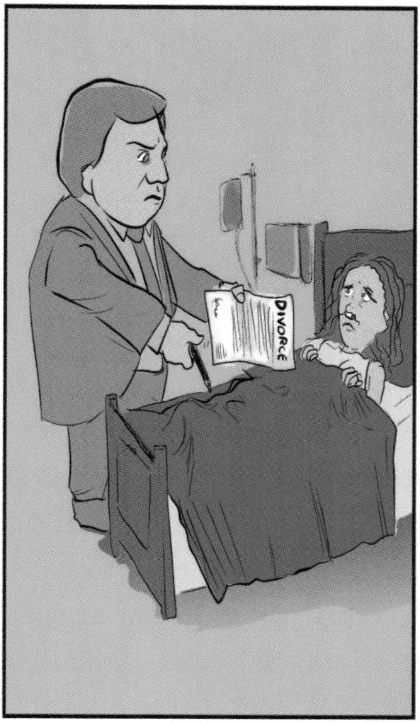
DIVORCE

July 12th, 2PM

Body language and physical appearance yield many cues as to a possible's status. In his best-selling book *Blink: The Power of Thinking Without Thinking*, Malcolm Gladwell asserts that we absorb important information about a person in the first two seconds of meeting or seeing him or her. We do a rapid cognition analysis that can be quite accurate. Initial reactions contain important information that is often ignored. For example, if you've just met someone and snaky images keep popping into your head, it may be for good reason. Listen to your instincts.

There is an antiquated tendency not to pay attention to rapid cognition cues, body language cues, or physical appearance cues when it comes to figures of authority. Public Level Bipedal Snakes who are charismatic or in an admired role hide in plain site, enabled by this 'don't be disrespectful' social habit. Since literally anyone can be a Bipedal Snake, a *set it and forget it* trust policy is unwise, no matter the person's station in society. As the illustration below infers: Just because someone's a doctor, that doesn't mean they're not a pervert too.

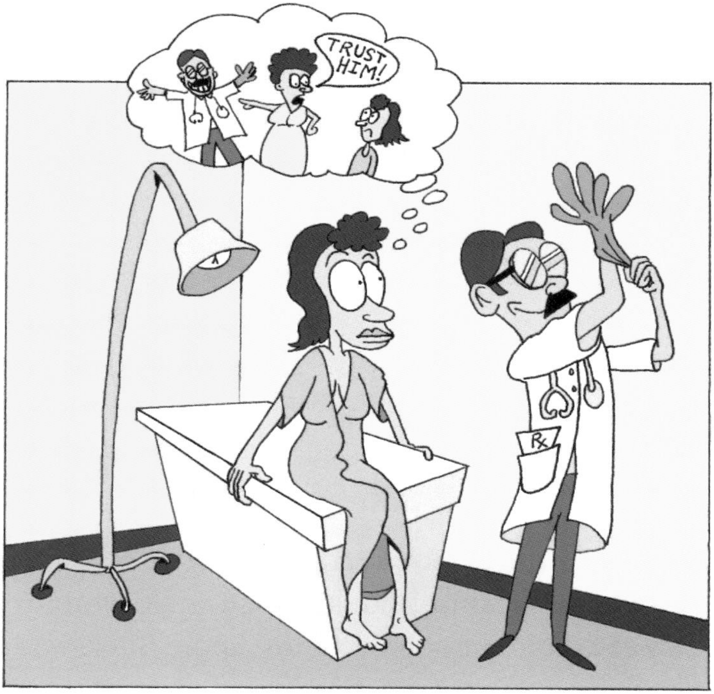
TRUST HIM!
Rx

Eye movement patterns also offer excellent snake-spotting opportunities. Dr. David Lieberman's book *Never be Lied to Again* explains that right-handed people will tend to look a bit up and to the right if they are engaging in memory retrieval thought (telling the truth) and up and to the left if they are engaging their creative thought centers (lying). The opposite is usually true for left-handed folks.

Determining if a person is truly snaky or not is often a matter of degree. Some people have a snaky trait or two but they're actually not a BS or an Apple Biter.

Visualize a machine like an optometrist might use for an eye examination. It has two round knobs on the examiner's side and a VU meter that runs latterly across the middle. The first knob can be turned from 0 to 11 and measures the level of inconsistency between a person's presentation of himself and the real things you know about him. The second knob can also be turned from 0 to 11, and it measures the ratio of snaky behaviors seen to the total amount of time you've observed the person.

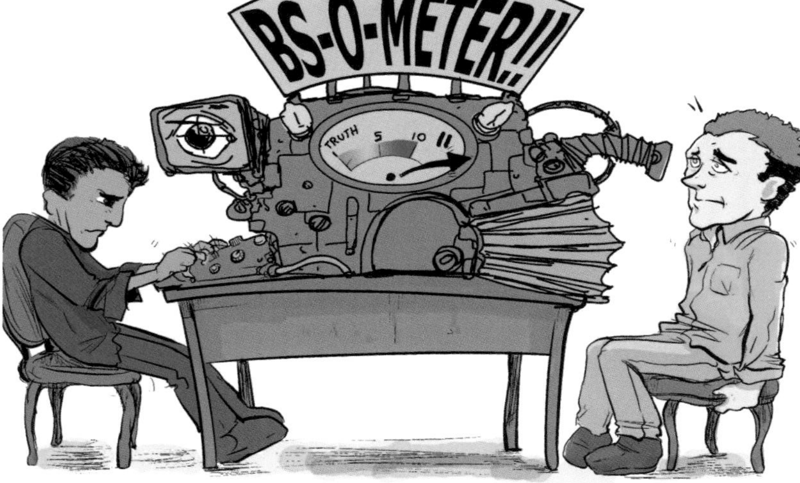
BS-O-METER!!
TRUTH
5
10
11

Both knobs grade low to high, so non-snaky is 0 and really snaky is 11. All points in between are relative shades of snakyness. After you set the knobs, the degree arrow will move right to left to indicate the snakyness level. If the arrow moves to 70 percent or higher, you've probably uncovered a BS. Be even more cautious if the possible snake you're applying the BS-O-Meter to is an Internet contact.

It's not a wise move to imbibe with BSs as they often become much more aggressive when inebriated. Conversely, your spotting skills become poorer, even though it might not feel like it. It may seem obvious, but lots of bites happen this way, particularly in the young clubbing population.

Another obvious and often overlooked point is not to allow yourself to be alone with a possible until you're confident you know who you're dealing with. Date rapes happen every day because of trusting too quickly. Our emotions may say "all clear" when the situation is anything but. Move slowly, cautiously, and don't just look at people's positive points. Being honest with yourself makes it easier to see a BS's games.

Relationships and Two Legged Snakes

Bipedal Snakes can be very charismatic and attractive. Emotional reactions to these qualities can have disastrous consequences if they're acted upon. The old axiom *just because you want to doesn't mean you should* was never more relevant because some Two Legged Snakes are incredibly seductive. The shining amorous light of a Decorated TLS in full bloom is one of the most tempting forces in nature. Their offer of pleasure stirs desire and creates mental confusion that compromises a potential bitee's power of decision making. John the Baptist lost his head because Salome's snaky dance was just too tempting for King Herod. Exotic dancer and courtesan Mata Hari seduced more than a few military secrets from the lips of her lovers before she was executed as a spy in 1941. And Spanish personality and actor Antonio Banderas sells many a bottle of his appropriately named fragrance *Seduction* because his bedroom eyes grace the packaging.

As hard as it is, if you're going to stand firm in the face of such gale force power you need to be able to tie yourself to the mast and wait out temptation's call.

Many people who have long histories of unhappy relationships are just poor BS spotters who move too quickly when it comes to romance. If those skills are improved and the attachment pace is slowed (the rate of emotional involvement compared to the amount of time the potential love interest has been known), a new personal life can quickly emerge.

To keep the pace of romantic involvement reasonable, limit the amount of time you spend with your potential love. It's much easier said than done but is wise nonetheless because BSs age poorly when the heat of the moment passes and the pheromone high abates.

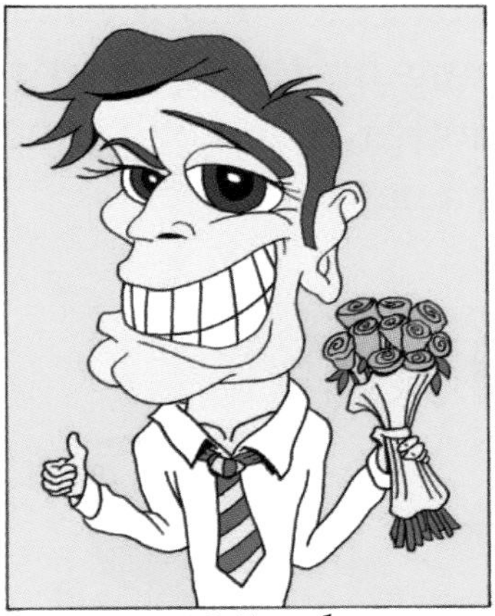

1 Month

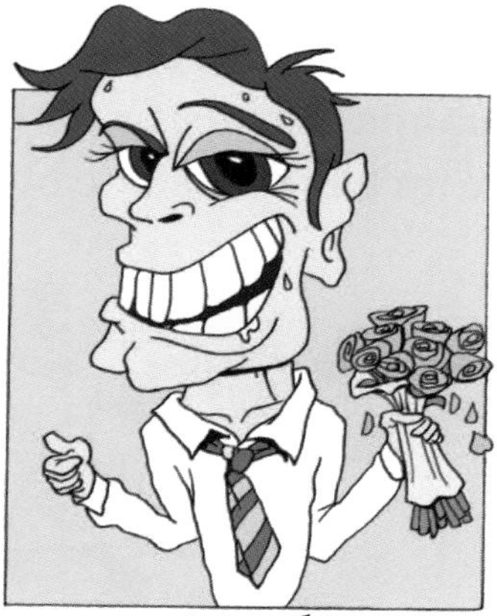

3 Months

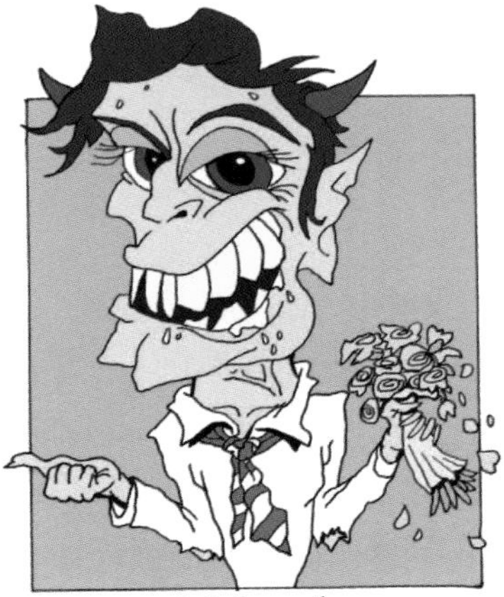

6 Months

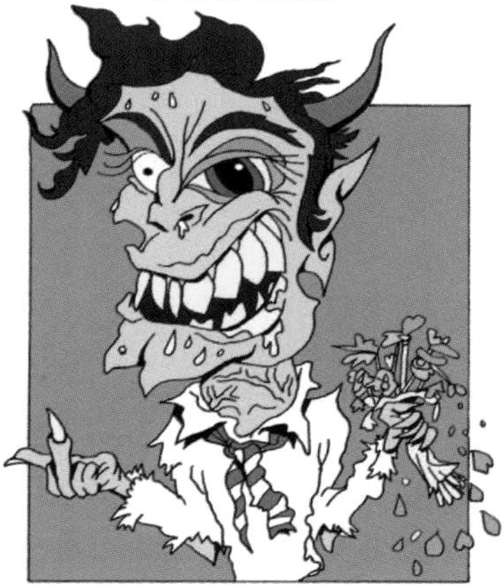

1 Year

Take heart in the fact that if your love is real and not the flames of a BS infatuation, you won't have lost any time with your love, you've just spread it out over a longer period. And if you avoided a BS involvement you've saved yourself a huge amount of pain ... or worse!

If you decide to throw caution to the wind and put a possible TLS on your lunchbox (give into a childish crush) you're likely to be signing up for a grand mal romantic disaster or perhaps another round of 'trying to cure an old snake bite by fixing a new snake.'

Many of us were severely snakebit as children. Our psyches protectively wrapped up the painful incidents and hid them in the back of our mental closets, the issues being simply too big to deal with at such a young age. At some point, when you're strong enough and in a supportive environment, these issues are best opened back up and dealt with so they don't cause continuing problems.

It's not unusual to hesitate, who would want to deal with all that old %^%$%^ if they didn't have to? But if those issues stay in the closet, negative compensations usually occur and that leads to even more suffering, for yourself and those around you.

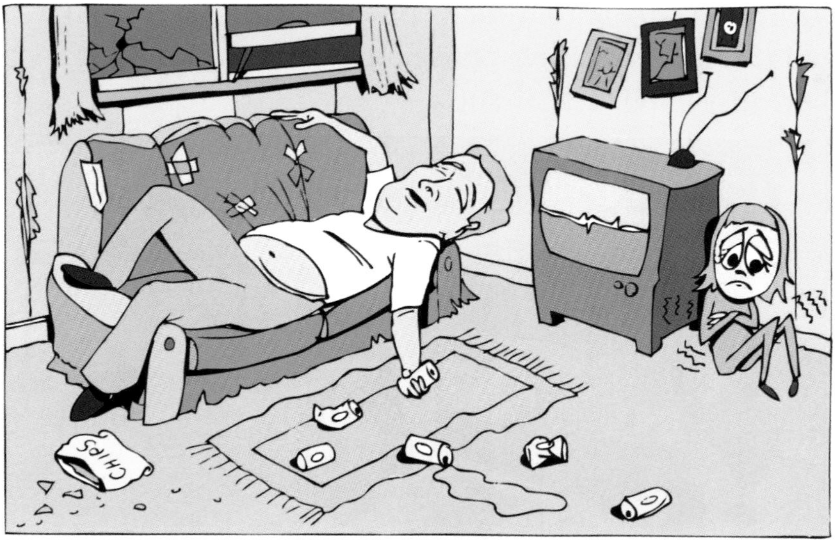
CHIPS

For example, picture a young girl named Bernice who was neglected and abused by an alcoholic father. She was too young to deal with the pain, fear, and anger she felt at the time, so she put it behind her and focused on school and then work.

Now she's a successful professional who on the outside has a great looking life, but she has a huge problem on the inside: she keeps dating losers who have alcohol or drug problems. She puts a lot of effort into helping them get better, and some seem to improve for a bit, but sooner or later they revert to their old ways, and this happens over and over. Bernice is caught in the painful cycle of 'trying to cure an old snake bite by fixing a new snake', a painful and repetitive consequence for not dealing with her early experience issues.

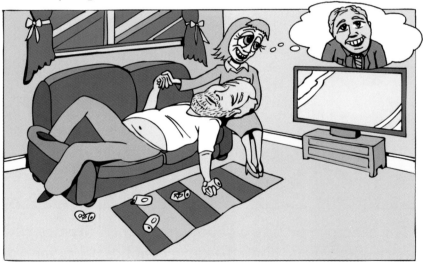

For some people awareness and making new choices is enough to get a new direction up and running. For others, social support groups like codependents anonymous are a wonderful information source and network that helps them change frustrating snake fixing habits. Professional help is another alternative that we'll discuss a bit later.

Family and Familiars

Most of us have snaky friends, coworkers, and family members that we cannot completely avoid. This gives us a lot of opportunities to perfect our snake handling skills. It could be someone like outside sales rep Tony, who always seems to have his hand out for a loan. You won't see him for months if you give in and you'll never get your money back unless he's setting you up for twice as much next time.

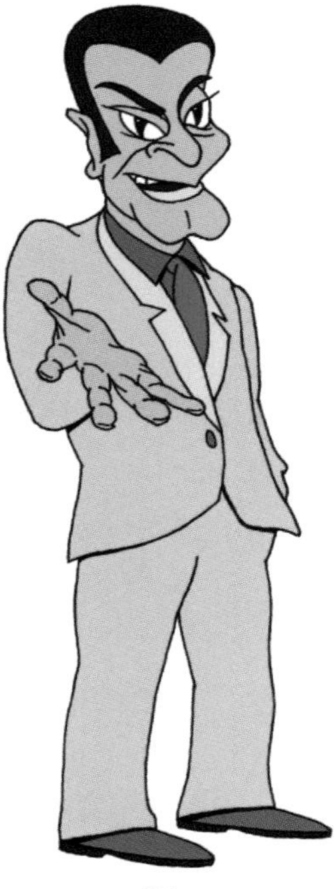

Tony

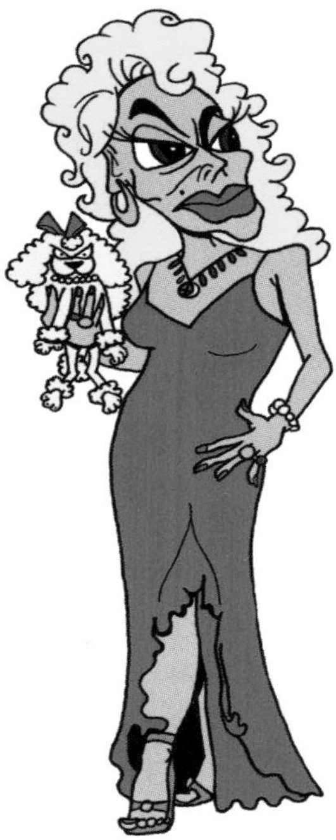

Aunt Elaine

Perhaps it's an Aunt Elaine from Los Angeles who talks about herself incessantly and has a really mean little dog. When she visits, everyone seems to be fighting all the time and your sister claims some of her jewelry is missing.

It could be a Grandpa Silas who scares everyone, and he seems to have elected you his 'snake in training'. His breath smells of cigarettes and bourbon and he wants you to sit on his lap while he talks about 'back in the day'.

We need to be honest about the areas in which our family members and other familiars are snaky and avoid dealing with them on that level. For example, if your cousin is a trash-talking, negative alliance-maker, just walk away when the judgmental slamming starts. Feign an intestinal issue if you have to. If a co-worker is snaky with money, avoid financial interactions with them at all costs. Firmly confront them if you need to, and don't capitulate if they starts begging sympathy or try to use other snaky persuasions. You can do it!

If you're chained to some really snaky family members or friends consider a 'three strikes and they're out' process. It's easy to describe but can be quite hard to do given the attachment and affection we feel for family and friends. But if they're going down you don't have to go down too, abandon ship!

To begin the 'three strikes' process confront the family members or friends with the snaky behaviors you're not going to continue to tolerate and try to come to some solution. Really put some effort into it and give it your best shot. If you don't find any sincere improvement or they won't listen at all, try twice more and then head for the door. You gave it your best, you can feel good about that. It's no use trying to change what you can't, that just leads to frustration and depression. Perhaps after some consequences they'll really get serious about changing their ways and you could give it another go, but don't count on it … the odds are against it.

A tough snaky situation, particularly in the context of family or familiars, is when someone you care about 'goes snake'. This isn't a Situational type of Bipedal Snake, this is a person you've known for a long time who hasn't previously been a TLS, going over to the snaky side. The reasons a person changes from being a trustable good egg to an un-trustable Two Legged Snake vary. Sometimes loss or grief will precipitate the snaky devolution. Other times it's a reaction to a person not measuring up to life's challenges and they're ashamed of themselves and feel they may as well give up by 'going snake'.

Many people who find new levels of success also find their old friends become snaky with jealously. Alcohol and drug problems can also lubricate a slide to snakedom. Whatever the reason be honest about the change as sad as it is, and practice the same protective measures you would if you were facing any other type of TLS.

If you have the urge to save your family or coworkers I urge you to ignore those impulses. Focus on your own spotting and handling skills and use attraction and modeling (leading by example), rather than promotion, to encourage a less serpentine path. Unsolicited assistance often entrenches and sometimes increases snaky behavior.

If you feel guilty about taking care of yourself and it persists, perhaps support groups like the aforementioned codependents anonymous or some professional help is a good idea. Don't feel ashamed, confronting the issues takes courage; appreciate your strength.

We're conditioned to accept almost anything in the name of family or friendship so it's hard to say good-bye. All that conditioning can lead you to feeling a lot of guilt when you say "no more." But it's you're life and not anyone else's, don't let guilt or avoidance call the shots.

In the *Peanuts* cartoon series Lucy keeps talking Charlie Brown into trying to kick the football and he always ends up on his back, betrayed again. Humorous as that cartoon is, getting repeatedly snakebit by family or friends isn't funny and can have disastrous consequences to you and you're family. Don't let a cage of TLSs pull you down, no matter who they are.

Having to deal with snaky behavior can be hard, so if you're having difficulties, don't get down on yourself, get help. Enlist the services of a professional personal coach or therapist. One who frequently works with people in the entertainment industry is usually a good choice. Look around until you're confident you've found someone who can help, and then give it a go.

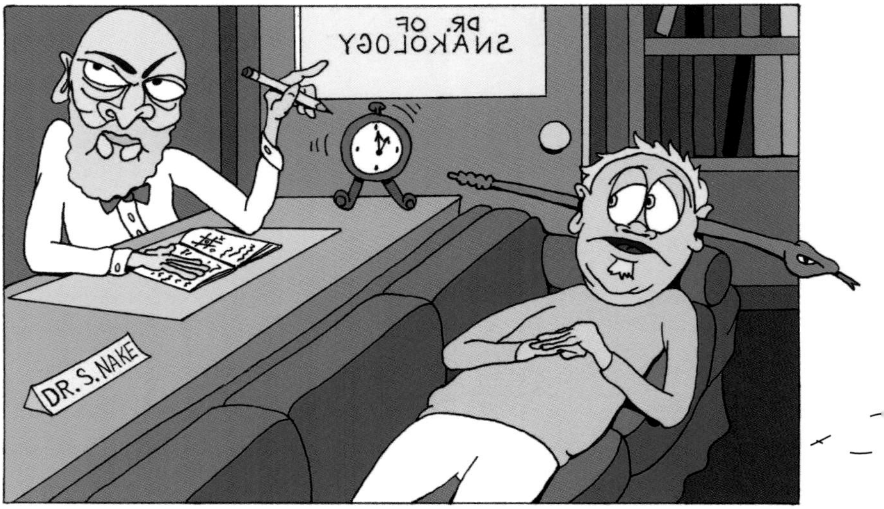
DR. OF SNAKOLOGY
DR. S. NAKE

If you do a few sessions and it doesn't feel right, go on the hunt for a new helper. Repeat until you find the right person. It often takes a while so don't give up. Your friends probably won't charge you to talk about issues with your snaky brethren, but if they haven't been bugging you about it already, it's likely they're also in a snake filled boat.

Continue to develop your sense of what's true and who's trustworthy by comparing how your initial judgments measure up to what you learn as time goes on. If your early judgments were not so good, try to figure out what you missed. Don't be afraid to look in the mirror for reasons. We're often susceptible to people and pitches we want to believe in because of what we want or need. BS spotting is an ever-growing skill set because Two Legged Snakes aren't going to stop coming up with new techniques anytime soon. With time, practice, and honest self-evaluation, most anyone can become an expert BS spotter.

I very much encourage you to keep this book handy and refer to it often, as rehearsal (going over and over things) helps your memory centers hold onto what you've learned. Turn your snake spotting and handling awareness into a lifelong snake spotting and handling tradition.

The Ladder of Friendship

When we build friendships and associations we normally engage in a back and forth series of interactions between ourselves and our potential friend. Picture two ladders side by side: As one person moves up on one of the ladders a rung at a time, the other person can either reciprocate and move up a rung on their ladder too, stay at the rung they're at, or perhaps pull back. This back and forth movement continues until a state of equilibrium or equal ladder level is established and a level of friendship is determined.

For instance, you notice someone at work and they seem pretty OK so you say "Hi" when you pass them in the hall. The next time you see the person they say "Hello" and you share a more formal introduction. The following meeting, you chat a bit and find out you both have an interest in baseball. Cool. Your next talk reveals that you're not aligned at all in terms of your religious views. Oh well. A level of friendship is determined by these to and fro movements; you have a friend at work that you like to talk sports with but you really don't see any reason to try to go farther because the religious differences would get in the way. That's a normal example of how friendship levels are determined using the ladder of trust analogy.

Two Legged Snakes move quite differently on the ladder of trust. All but the most sophisticated will move up too quickly jumping several rungs at a time. Others will be jerky and move up and down in sharp jagged bursts. If you notice these kinds of movements be cautious about investing trust in that person, as they may not be looking for the right friendship balance, but the right time to bite.

Bipedal Snake Experts

Many families, workplaces, and social circles have their resident BS experts. Most are a bit full of themselves and create a wave of eye rolling when they take the tone of voice that indicates 'here we go again'. Besides mentioning their degree or title too often, their main 'tell' is the overuse of superfluous "facts." Trivial and non-trivial fodder that really isn't necessary will be paraded out to establish them as 'an expert in the field'. If we're talking science, way too much data will be presented. In the realm of religion, the Bible, Quran, or Torah will be over quoted in an attempt to 'smoke and mirror' the audience into accepting their precepts. Physicist Richard Feynman said, "if you can't explain it to a six-year-old, you don't know what you're talking about." While some subjects make this a stretch, real experts aren't trying to baffle you with BS, they're sincerely trying to communicate their points. The difference between a true expert and a BS artist isn't hard to see, if you know what to look for.

The Snakes in Our Heads

Even if you grew up in a snake-free home environment, BS marketing strategists have been working to get into your head since early childhood with associations, suggestions and outright lies. On the D2D level BSs are currently so prevalent that it would seem impossible to not be touched by their influence. With all the BSing that's about it's easy for a really good person to still have some pretty snaky thoughts and beliefs rattling around in their head.

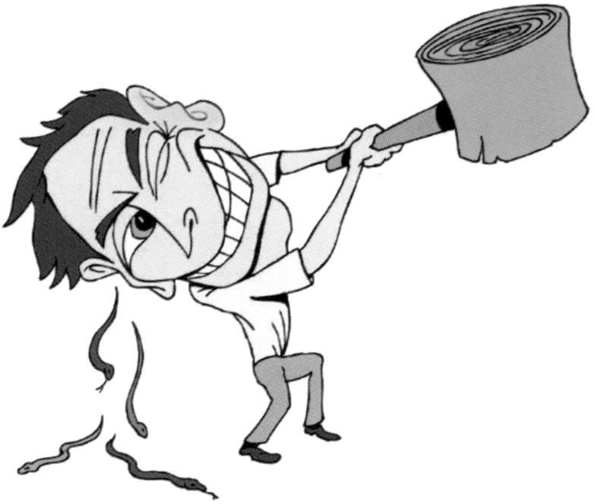

The cure for 'snake head' isn't difficult, doesn't entail an expensive course of BS debriefing therapy, and doesn't require your subscription to some culty belief system. The cure is simply to learn to think for yourself and decide what (non-snaky) thoughts and actions you want to make a habit of and what (snaky) beliefs and reactions you want to get rid of. Of course your snake spotting and handling skills and knowledge of snaky techniques will be very useful.

Take 15 to 20 minutes each day to honestly and openly reflect on your actions, reactions, emotions, and thoughts (in a hot tub isn't a bad way to go). You'll learn a lot about yourself pretty quickly (and no, smoking pot does not help the self reflective process!). As you think about your day what do you see as possibly snaky in your actions, reactions, emotions and thoughts? Were these things necessary or were they a bit of snaky conditioning that you need to correct? Think about what you'd rather do and then picture yourself doing that and feeling good about it. Repeat, repeat, repeat until it sticks.

There are several steps to self-correcting away from BSness. The first is of course awareness; we can't very well solve a problem if we don't know it's there. The second step is to select an appropriate alternative (the right way to do things) and the third step is: practice, practice, practice. A good way to remind yourself of what you're working to change is to put 'reminder' objects around the house. If you're working on being more assertive with snaky individuals, a refrigerator magnet of a gorilla could help keep you on top of your program. If you've gotten in the snaky habit of trusting too quickly a Captain Denial Dave coffee cup might help you remember to take your time figuring out who's trustable, so you don't have to sink or swim. Visit www.twoleggedsnakes. com and peruse the merchandise; you may find a good reminder there or create your own through our interactive connection with www.zazzle.com.

When you're creating new thought and behavioral patterns have patience, it takes more than a few repetitions to establish a new habit pattern. If you string about twenty consecutive new patterns together that should be enough to replace the old habit, but the numbers vary a lot between different people and issues, so keep at it even if it takes a hundred.

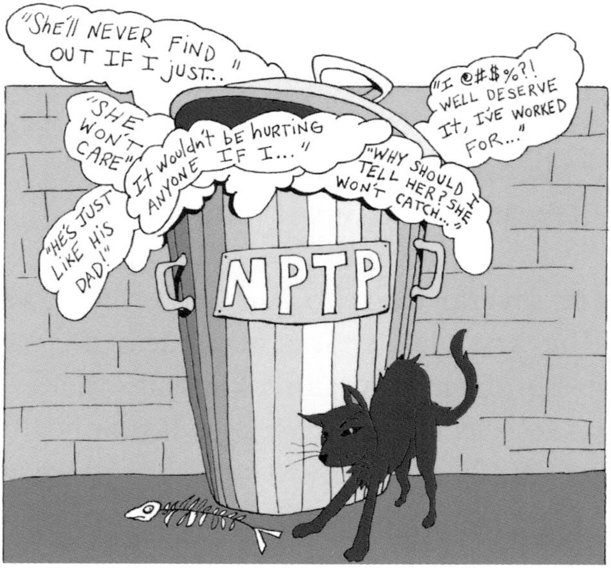
"SHE'll NEVER FIND OUT IF I JUST..."
"SHE WON'T CARE"
It wouldn't be hurting ANYONE IF I..."
"I @#$%?! WELL DESERVE It, I'VE WORKED FOR..."
"WHY SHOULD I TELL HER? SHE WON'T CATCH..."
"HE'S JUST LIKE HIS DAD!"
NPTP

In the Far East there is a popular saying: "the mind is like a monkey stung by a scorpion babbling all the time." You'll undoubtedly encounter that monkey when you start your process of self-reflection. He'll be directing you to think about what's going on sale at Macys or whose likely to win the big game on Sunday rather than on your intended focus of 'to snake or not to snake ...' Try to stay on a productive thought pattern course and put non-productive thought patterns in a NPTP garbage can.

There's an acquisition curve to new behavior patterns that's useful in mapping your progress. After you've established your new behavior or thought pattern goal, you'll find that at first you still automatically continue with the old pattern. You won't even think of the new behavioral goal until some time after an old pattern 'occasion'. As you progress you'll find you're thinking of your new pattern more and more closely to the occasions of continuing with the old. It may seem a bit strange but old habits can take awhile to die. During the next stage you'll be engaged in the old pattern and aware of the new one simultaneously and you'll probably be in a bit of a mental tussle. Finally your goal will start winning out and you'll string together longer and longer repetitions of the new pattern. When you get to twenty or so the new pattern will be automatic and awareness of the old pattern will fade until it is forgotten. Now the new pattern is established and you're more yourself than before because you're doing as you've chosen, not what your conditioning experience directs you to do.

Take Bill, for example, a likable 40ish fellow who discovers through the process of self-reflection that he has a snaky habit of automatically lying to people. The words are out of his mouth before he even realizes it. The reason he lies seems to be to get people to like him, as they're lies that make him look good or successful in some way. It doesn't really work because if people do like him it's only his act they like and many times he's gotten caught lying and those were embarrassing, shameful experiences.

His goal is to tell the truth; it's fine to put things in a favorable light but no more outright fabrications. At first it was days before he'd recognize instances when he'd lied, however the daily reflections helped and he got quicker and quicker at recognizing his snaky behaviors, after the fact. The stage of simultaneously recognizing the need for the new truthful pattern and the lie coming out of his mouth was rough, and he had more than a few stammering, embarrassing moments, but he held on and was able to start stringing incidents of his new truthfulness together. After a few relapses he made it to about twenty consecutive repetitions and his new pattern of telling (the best version of) the truth was in place. The days of his automatic lying are now a mere memory.

The goal of self-reflection is to purge the snaky patterns that were trained into you and help you reclaim yourself. The additional benefits of having a more prosperous and enjoyable life and perhaps finding ways to positively contribute are also common experiences of those who have transcended the snakes in their heads. It's a great feeling to share what you've learned with receptive people and it also has the side benefit of helping you hang onto your hard-earned wisdom.

Sometimes it seems like everyone in the world is too snaky to trust. Of course that's not true but the current BS 'bloom' can make it feel that way. Take your time building your relationships and be honest with yourself about what you see. That'll give you the best chance possible of having a snake-free social life. Visit our social networking site at www.facebook.com/twoleggedsnakes; you may meet some new non-snaky friends there.

> " It is better to learn the
> ways of those who would
> bite us and prevent it,
> than let biting grow to
> be the way of the world. "

To bite or not to bite.

That is the question.

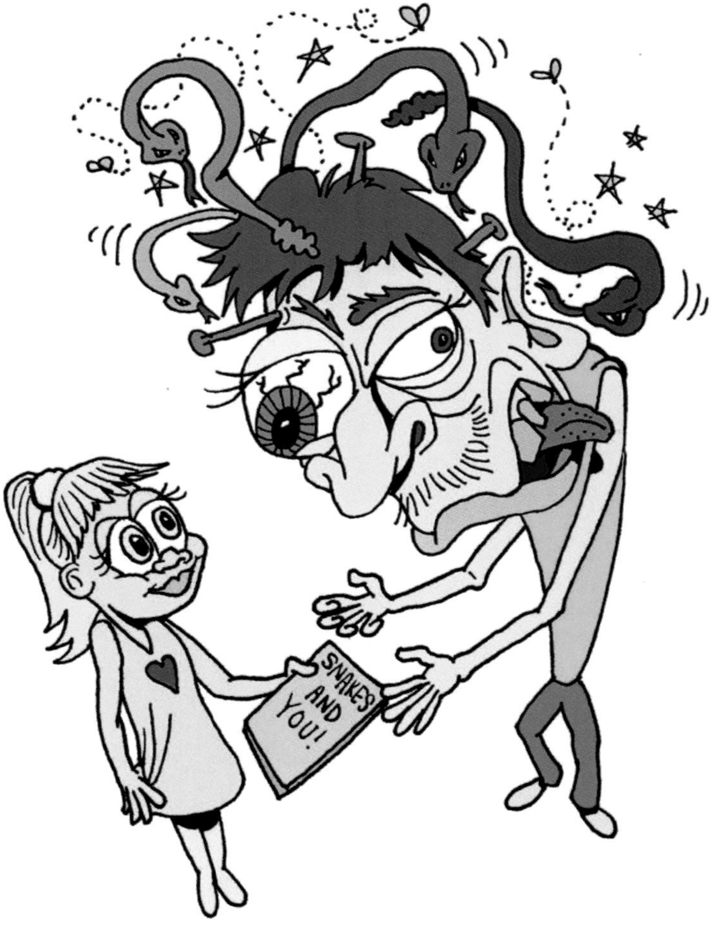
SNAKES AND YOU!

P.S. When your snake spotting and handling skills become second nature, please feel free to give this book to friends, family, and others who are struggling with BSs or their own snaky behavior (anonymously is fine). Highlighting the most important bits may help get the message across.

A special thanks goes to Mrs. Joyce Engelson for her wonderful sense of humor and insightful feedback. Without her encouragement, this project wouldn't have gotten off the ground.

Illustration and Design Team

Donny Smutz is credited for the illustrations on pages 3, 7, 8, 9, 10, 14, 15, 19, 20, 21, 22, 25, 28, 32, 33, 35, 37, 41, 42, 43, 45, 47, 48, 54, 55, 56, 58, 59, 60, 62, 66, 68, 73, 76, 78, 79, 82, 83, 85, 86, 87, 88, 89, 90, 93, 94, 98, 100, 103, 104, 106.

Donny Smutz is an illustrator and frequently controversial visual artist. His work has been featured in *Juxtapoz* and *Nashville Arts* maga- zines, among others. He currently resides and

works in Nashville, TN, and can be contacted at dsmutz@twoleggedsnakes.com.

Sherard Jackson is credited for the illustrations on pages 4, 5, 6, 12, 13, 15, 16, 17, 23, 24, 26, 27, 29, 30, 31, 33, 34, 36, 38, 39, 40, 44, 46, 50, 51, 52, 53, 57, 61, 63, 64, 65, 67, 69, 74, 75, 77, 80, 81, 95, 111, 112.

Sherard Jackson is an illustrator and animator. He has produced illustrations for Image Com- ics, Antarctic Press, BOOM! Studios, Hasbro, White Wolf Inc, Big Head Press, and Roxor Games. His feature film credits include animation on *A Scan- ner Darkly*(2005), and *Flatland: the Movie*(2006). He currently resides and works as a freelance artist in Nashville, TN, and can be contacted at sjackson@twoleggedsnakes.com.

Patrick Schlafer is the book designer for *Two Legged Snakes: Understanding and Handling Manipulative People.* He is an artist and free- lance designer currently working and resid- ing in Nashville, TN. He can be contacted at pschlafer@twoleggedsnakes.com.

Log on to **www.twoleggedsnakes.com** and use code *1mor4me* to download your bonus chapter, *How Two Legged Snakes Almost Caused the Second Great Depression.*

Bibliography

Gladwell, Malcolm. *Blink: The Power of Thinking Without Thinking.* New York: Little, Brown & Company, 2005.

Hartly, Gregory & Karinch, Maryann. *How to Spot a Liar.* Franklin Lakes, NJ: Career Press, 2005.

Lieberman, David J., Ph.D. *Never Be Lied To Again.* New York: St. Martins Griffin, 1998.

Taleb, Nassim Nicholas. *The Black Swan: The Impact of the Highly Improbable.* New York: Random House, Inc., 2007.

Toffler, Alvin. *Future Shock.* New York: Bantam Books, 1970.

Two Legged Snake Spotters Checklist

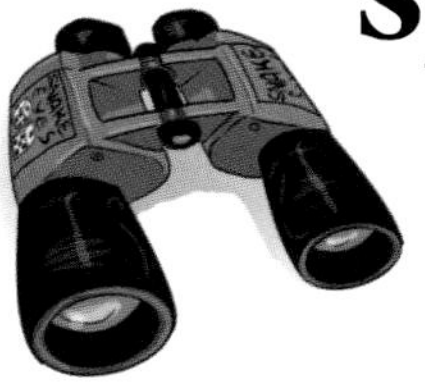

POSSIBLE SNAKE'S NAME/ID CODE: ______________

OBSERVATION DATES: __________________________

SOCIAL LEVEL: ☐ D2D ☐ PBS

POSSIBLE SNAKE TYPES (CHECK ALL THAT MAY APPLY): ☐ The Charmer ☐ Backstabber
☐ Bombast Entertainer ☐ Bilker ☐ Decorated
☐ Misdirector ☐ Rhetorical ☐ Situational
☐ Media Maven ☐ Lost ☐ Lifer ☐ Justified
☐ King Cobra ☐ Transcendent
☐ Other (define attributes) __________________

POSSIBLE FAN TYPE: ☐ True Believer ☐ WannaBe
☐ Follow the Leader ☐ Loyalists
☐ Other (define attributes) __________________

PERSAUASIVE TECHNIQUES OBSERVER:
☐ Accusination ☐ Misdirection ☐ Misassociation
☐ Going Big ☐ Disproportioning
☐ Rave-Up Questioning ☐ Burlesquing
☐ Bombasting ☐ Viperation ☐ Overtalking
☐ Demanding ☐ Begging Sympathy ☐ Flattery
☐ Yes Setting ☐ Reinventing History
☐ Other (define attributes)__________________

BITING STYLE OBSERVED: ☐ The Nibbler
☐ The Chomper ☐ The Pouncer

Communication Style: ☐ Logical ☐ Rationalizing
☐ Passionate ☐ Pseudo-intellectual
☐ Bible Beater ☐ Hothead ☐ Leader ☐ Smarmy
☐ Too Polite ☐ Aloof ☐ Charming
☐ Too Touchy ☐ Looney
☐ Other ______________________________

Appearance: ☐ Casual/Stylish ☐ Casual/Sloppy
☐ Polished/Professional ☐ Overpolished
☐ Dirtbag ☐ Hot! Hot! Hot! ☐ Severe
☐ Other ______________________________

Initial 'Blink' Reactions: ☐ Hmmm… ☐ Ugh!
☐ Hello Gorgeous… ☐ Run! ☐ Other ________

Pace(s) Observed: ☐ Slow ☐ Medium ☐ Fast
☐ Superfast ☐ Other ____________________

Eye Movements: ☐ Jittery ☐ Long Holds
☐ Up to Right ☐ Up to Left ☐ Back and Forth

Consistency Observed: Does this Possible's presentation match what you know about them?
☐ Yes, absolutely ☐ For the most part
☐ Not so much ☐ Not at all

Does this person do what they say and say what they do? ☐ Always ☐ Mostly
☐ Sometimes ☐ Eh… ☐ Never

Observer Analysis: Are you taking your time?
☐ Yes ☐ No, why not? __________________

Do you want to jump this person's bones, fix them, or fight them? ☐ Yes ☐ No ☐ Maybe

Overall TLS danger rating: ______________

Recommendations and comments:

____

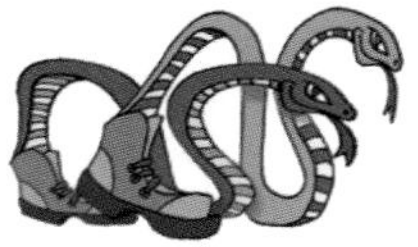

Two Legged Snake Spotters Checklist

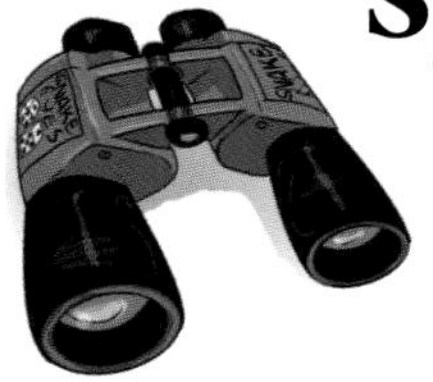

Possible Snake's Name/ID code: ______________

Observation Dates: ______________________

Social Level: ☐ D2D ☐ PBS

Possible Snake Types (Check all that may apply): ☐ The Charmer ☐ Backstabber
☐ Bombast Entertainer ☐ Bilker ☐ Decorated
☐ Misdirector ☐ Rhetorical ☐ Situational
☐ Media Maven ☐ Lost ☐ Lifer ☐ Justified
☐ King Cobra ☐ Transcendent
☐ Other (define attributes) ______________

Possible Fan Type: ☐ True Believer ☐ WannaBe
☐ Follow the Leader ☐ Loyalists
☐ Other (define attributes) ______________

Persauasive Techniques Observer:
☐ Accusination ☐ Misdirection ☐ Misassociation
☐ Going Big ☐ Disproportioning
☐ Rave-Up Questioning ☐ Burlesquing
☐ Bombasting ☐ Viperation ☐ Overtalking
☐ Demanding ☐ Begging Sympathy ☐ Flattery
☐ Yes Setting ☐ Reinventing History
☐ Other (define attributes)______________

Biting Style Observed: ☐ The Nibbler
☐ The Chomper ☐ The Pouncer

Communication Style: ☐ Logical ☐ Rationalizing
☐ Passionate ☐ Pseudo-intellectual
☐ Bible Beater ☐ Hothead ☐ Leader ☐ Smarmy
☐ Too Polite ☐ Aloof ☐ Charming
☐ Too Touchy ☐ Looney
☐ Other ______________________________

Appearance: ☐ Casual/Stylish ☐ Casual/Sloppy
☐ Polished/Professional ☐ Overpolished
☐ Dirtbag ☐ Hot! Hot! Hot! ☐ Severe
☐ Other ______________________________

Initial 'Blink' Reactions: ☐ Hmmm… ☐ Ugh!
☐ Hello Gorgeous… ☐ Run! ☐ Other ________

Pace(s) Observed: ☐ Slow ☐ Medium ☐ Fast
☐ Superfast ☐ Other ____________________

Eye Movements: ☐ Jittery ☐ Long Holds
☐ Up to Right ☐ Up to Left ☐ Back and Forth

Consistency Observed: Does this Possible's presentation match what you know about them?
☐ Yes, absolutely ☐ For the most part
☐ Not so much ☐ Not at all

Does this person do what they say and say what they do? ☐ Always ☐ Mostly
☐ Sometimes ☐ Eh… ☐ Never

- - - - - - - - - - - - -

Observer Analysis: Are you taking your time?
☐ Yes ☐ No, why not? __________________

Do you want to jump this person's bones, fix them, or fight them? ☐ Yes ☐ No ☐ Maybe

Overall TLS danger rating: ______________

Recommendations and comments:

____

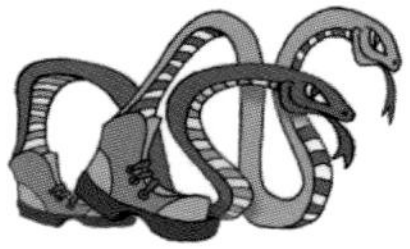

Two Legged Snake Spotters Checklist

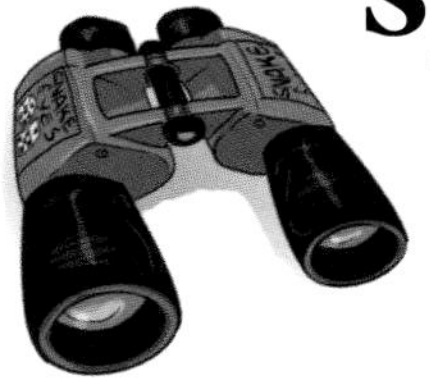
SNAKE EYES

Possible Snake's Name/ID code: ______________

Observation Dates: __________________________

Social Level: ❑ D2D ❑ PBS

Possible Snake Types (check all that may apply): ❑ The Charmer ❑ Backstabber
❑ Bombast Entertainer ❑ Bilker ❑ Decorated
❑ Misdirector ❑ Rhetorical ❑ Situational
❑ Media Maven ❑ Lost ❑ Lifer ❑ Justified
❑ King Cobra ❑ Transcendent
❑ Other (define attributes) __________________

Possible Fan Type: ❑ True Believer ❑ WannaBe
❑ Follow the Leader ❑ Loyalists
❑ Other (define attributes) __________________

Persauasive Techniques Observer:
❑ Accusination ❑ Misdirection ❑ Misassociation
❑ Going Big ❑ Disproportioning
❑ Rave-Up Questioning ❑ Burlesquing
❑ Bombasting ❑ Viperation ❑ Overtalking
❑ Demanding ❑ Begging Sympathy ❑ Flattery
❑ Yes Setting ❑ Reinventing History
❑ Other (define attributes)__________________

Biting Style Observed: ❑ The Nibbler
❑ The Chomper ❑ The Pouncer

Communication Style: ☐ Logical ☐ Rationalizing
☐ Passionate ☐ Pseudo-intellectual
☐ Bible Beater ☐ Hothead ☐ Leader ☐ Smarmy
☐ Too Polite ☐ Aloof ☐ Charming
☐ Too Touchy ☐ Looney
☐ Other ______________________________

Appearance: ☐ Casual/Stylish ☐ Casual/Sloppy
☐ Polished/Professional ☐ Overpolished
☐ Dirtbag ☐ Hot! Hot! Hot! ☐ Severe
☐ Other ______________________________

Initial 'Blink' Reactions: ☐ Hmmm… ☐ Ugh!
☐ Hello Gorgeous… ☐ Run! ☐ Other ________

Pace(s) Observed: ☐ Slow ☐ Medium ☐ Fast
☐ Superfast ☐ Other ____________________

Eye Movements: ☐ Jittery ☐ Long Holds
☐ Up to Right ☐ Up to Left ☐ Back and Forth

Consistency Observed: Does this Possible's presentation match what you know about them?
☐ Yes, absolutely ☐ For the most part
☐ Not so much ☐ Not at all

Does this person do what they say and say what they do? ☐ Always ☐ Mostly
☐ Sometimes ☐ Eh… ☐ Never

Observer Analysis: Are you taking your time?
☐ Yes ☐ No, why not? __________________

Do you want to jump this person's bones, fix them, or fight them? ☐ Yes ☐ No ☐ Maybe

Overall TLS danger rating: ________________

Recommendations and comments:

____

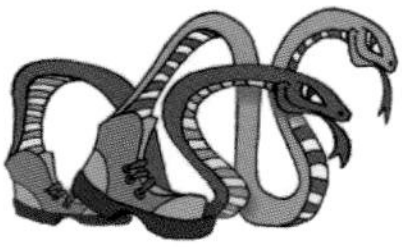

Two Legged Snake Spotters Checklist

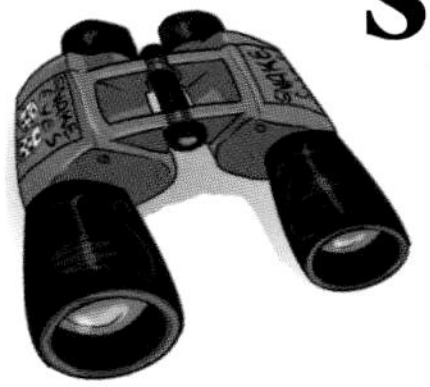

Possible Snake's Name/ID code: ______________

Observation Dates: __________________________

Social Level: ☐ D2D ☐ PBS

Possible Snake Types (Check all that may apply): ☐ The Charmer ☐ Backstabber
☐ Bombast Entertainer ☐ Bilker ☐ Decorated
☐ Misdirector ☐ Rhetorical ☐ Situational
☐ Media Maven ☐ Lost ☐ Lifer ☐ Justified
☐ King Cobra ☐ Transcendent
☐ Other (define attributes) __________________

Possible Fan Type: ☐ True Believer ☐ WannaBe
☐ Follow the Leader ☐ Loyalists
☐ Other (define attributes) __________________

Persauasive Techniques Observer:
☐ Accusination ☐ Misdirection ☐ Misassociation
☐ Going Big ☐ Disproportioning
☐ Rave-Up Questioning ☐ Burlesquing
☐ Bombasting ☐ Viperation ☐ Overtalking
☐ Demanding ☐ Begging Sympathy ☐ Flattery
☐ Yes Setting ☐ Reinventing History
☐ Other (define attributes)___________________

Biting Style Observed: ☐ The Nibbler
☐ The Chomper ☐ The Pouncer

Communication Style: ☐ Logical ☐ Rationalizing
☐ Passionate ☐ Pseudo-intellectual
☐ Bible Beater ☐ Hothead ☐ Leader ☐ Smarmy
☐ Too Polite ☐ Aloof ☐ Charming
☐ Too Touchy ☐ Looney
☐ Other ______________________

Appearance: ☐ Casual/Stylish ☐ Casual/Sloppy
☐ Polished/Professional ☐ Overpolished
☐ Dirtbag ☐ Hot! Hot! Hot! ☐ Severe
☐ Other ______________________

Initial 'Blink' Reactions: ☐ Hmmm… ☐ Ugh!
☐ Hello Gorgeous… ☐ Run! ☐ Other ________

Pace(s) Observed: ☐ Slow ☐ Medium ☐ Fast
☐ Superfast ☐ Other ______________

Eye Movements: ☐ Jittery ☐ Long Holds
☐ Up to Right ☐ Up to Left ☐ Back and Forth

Consistency Observed: Does this Possible's presentation match what you know about them?
☐ Yes, absolutely ☐ For the most part
☐ Not so much ☐ Not at all

Does this person do what they say and say what they do? ☐ Always ☐ Mostly
☐ Sometimes ☐ Eh… ☐ Never

- - - - - - - - - - - - -

Observer Analysis: Are you taking your time?
☐ Yes ☐ No, why not? ______________

Do you want to jump this person's bones, fix them, or fight them? ☐ Yes ☐ No ☐ Maybe

Overall TLS danger rating: ______________

Recommendations and comments:

____

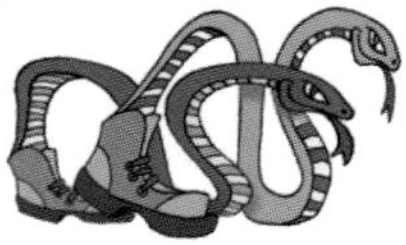

Two Legged Snake Spotters Checklist

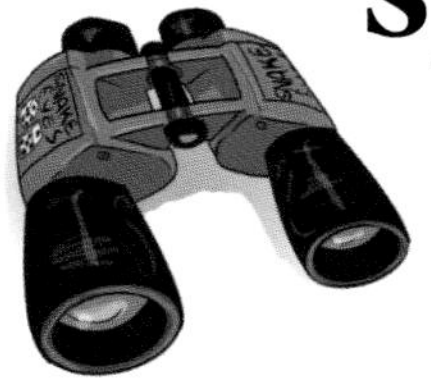
SNAKE

Possible Snake's Name/ID code: ______________

Observation Dates: ________________________

Social Level: ☐ D2D ☐ PBS

Possible Snake Types (Check all that may apply): ☐ The Charmer ☐ Backstabber
☐ Bombast Entertainer ☐ Bilker ☐ Decorated
☐ Misdirector ☐ Rhetorical ☐ Situational
☐ Media Maven ☐ Lost ☐ Lifer ☐ Justified
☐ King Cobra ☐ Transcendent
☐ Other (define attributes) _________________

Possible Fan Type: ☐ True Believer ☐ WannaBe
☐ Follow the Leader ☐ Loyalists
☐ Other (define attributes) _________________

Persauasive Techniques Observer:
☐ Accusination ☐ Misdirection ☐ Misassociation
☐ Going Big ☐ Disproportioning
☐ Rave-Up Questioning ☐ Burlesquing
☐ Bombasting ☐ Viperation ☐ Overtalking
☐ Demanding ☐ Begging Sympathy ☐ Flattery
☐ Yes Setting ☐ Reinventing History
☐ Other (define attributes)_________________

Biting Style Observed: ☐ The Nibbler
☐ The Chomper ☐ The Pouncer

Communication Style: ☐ Logical ☐ Rationalizing
☐ Passionate ☐ Pseudo-intellectual
☐ Bible Beater ☐ Hothead ☐ Leader ☐ Smarmy
☐ Too Polite ☐ Aloof ☐ Charming
☐ Too Touchy ☐ Looney
☐ Other ______________________________

Appearance: ☐ Casual/Stylish ☐ Casual/Sloppy
☐ Polished/Professional ☐ Overpolished
☐ Dirtbag ☐ Hot! Hot! Hot! ☐ Severe
☐ Other ______________________________

Initial 'Blink' Reactions: ☐ Hmmm… ☐ Ugh!
☐ Hello Gorgeous… ☐ Run! ☐ Other ________

Pace(s) Observed: ☐ Slow ☐ Medium ☐ Fast
☐ Superfast ☐ Other ____________________

Eye Movements: ☐ Jittery ☐ Long Holds
☐ Up to Right ☐ Up to Left ☐ Back and Forth

Consistency Observed: Does this Possible's presentation match what you know about them?
☐ Yes, absolutely ☐ For the most part
☐ Not so much ☐ Not at all

Does this person do what they say and say what they do? ☐ Always ☐ Mostly
☐ Sometimes ☐ Eh… ☐ Never

Observer Analysis: Are you taking your time?
☐ Yes ☐ No, why not? __________________

Do you want to jump this person's bones, fix them, or fight them? ☐ Yes ☐ No ☐ Maybe

Overall TLS danger rating: ______________

Recommendations and comments:

____

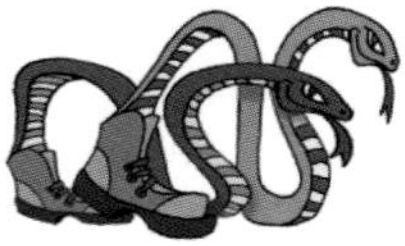

Two Legged Snake Spotters Checklist

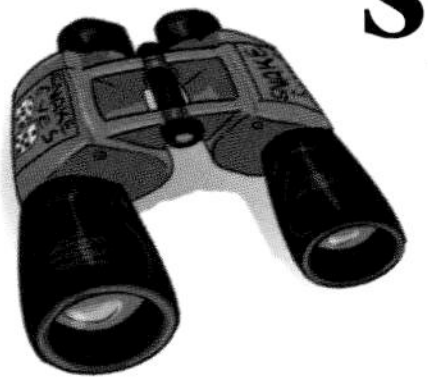

Possible Snake's Name/ID code: ______________

Observation Dates: __________________________

Social Level: ☐ D2D ☐ PBS

Possible Snake Types (Check all that may apply): ☐ The Charmer ☐ Backstabber
☐ Bombast Entertainer ☐ Bilker ☐ Decorated
☐ Misdirector ☐ Rhetorical ☐ Situational
☐ Media Maven ☐ Lost ☐ Lifer ☐ Justified
☐ King Cobra ☐ Transcendent
☐ Other (define attributes) __________________

Possible Fan Type: ☐ True Believer ☐ WannaBe
☐ Follow the Leader ☐ Loyalists
☐ Other (define attributes) __________________

Persauasive Techniques Observer:
☐ Accusination ☐ Misdirection ☐ Misassociation
☐ Going Big ☐ Disproportioning
☐ Rave-Up Questioning ☐ Burlesquing
☐ Bombasting ☐ Viperation ☐ Overtalking
☐ Demanding ☐ Begging Sympathy ☐ Flattery
☐ Yes Setting ☐ Reinventing History
☐ Other (define attributes)__________________

Biting Style Observed: ☐ The Nibbler
☐ The Chomper ☐ The Pouncer

Communication Style: ☐ Logical ☐ Rationalizing
☐ Passionate ☐ Pseudo-intellectual
☐ Bible Beater ☐ Hothead ☐ Leader ☐ Smarmy
☐ Too Polite ☐ Aloof ☐ Charming
☐ Too Touchy ☐ Looney
☐ Other ___________________________

Appearance: ☐ Casual/Stylish ☐ Casual/Sloppy
☐ Polished/Professional ☐ Overpolished
☐ Dirtbag ☐ Hot! Hot! Hot! ☐ Severe
☐ Other ___________________________

Initial 'Blink' Reactions: ☐ Hmmm… ☐ Ugh!
☐ Hello Gorgeous… ☐ Run! ☐ Other ________

Pace(s) Observed: ☐ Slow ☐ Medium ☐ Fast
☐ Superfast ☐ Other ________________

Eye Movements: ☐ Jittery ☐ Long Holds
☐ Up to Right ☐ Up to Left ☐ Back and Forth

Consistency Observed: Does this Possible's presentation match what you know about them?
☐ Yes, absolutely ☐ For the most part
☐ Not so much ☐ Not at all

Does this person do what they say and say what they do? ☐ Always ☐ Mostly
☐ Sometimes ☐ Eh… ☐ Never

Observer Analysis: Are you taking your time?
☐ Yes ☐ No, why not? ________________

Do you want to jump this person's bones, fix them, or fight them? ☐ Yes ☐ No ☐ Maybe

Overall TLS danger rating: ________________

Recommendations and comments:

____

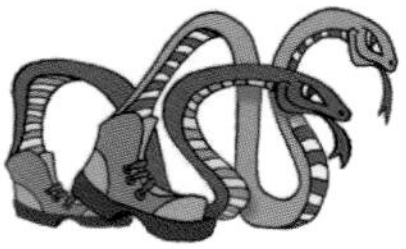

Two Legged Snake Spotters Checklist

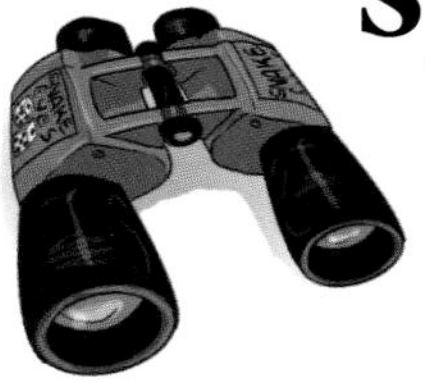
SNAKE

Possible Snake's Name/ID code: ______________

Observation Dates: ______________________

Social Level: ☐ D2D ☐ PBS

Possible Snake Types (Check all that may apply): ☐ The Charmer ☐ Backstabber
☐ Bombast Entertainer ☐ Bilker ☐ Decorated
☐ Misdirector ☐ Rhetorical ☐ Situational
☐ Media Maven ☐ Lost ☐ Lifer ☐ Justified
☐ King Cobra ☐ Transcendent
☐ Other (define attributes) ________________

Possible Fan Type: ☐ True Believer ☐ WannaBe
☐ Follow the Leader ☐ Loyalists
☐ Other (define attributes) ________________

Persauasive Techniques Observer:
☐ Accusination ☐ Misdirection ☐ Misassociation
☐ Going Big ☐ Disproportioning
☐ Rave-Up Questioning ☐ Burlesquing
☐ Bombasting ☐ Viperation ☐ Overtalking
☐ Demanding ☐ Begging Sympathy ☐ Flattery
☐ Yes Setting ☐ Reinventing History
☐ Other (define attributes)________________

Biting Style Observed: ☐ The Nibbler
☐ The Chomper ☐ The Pouncer

Communication Style: ☐ Logical ☐ Rationalizing
☐ Passionate ☐ Pseudo-intellectual
☐ Bible Beater ☐ Hothead ☐ Leader ☐ Smarmy
☐ Too Polite ☐ Aloof ☐ Charming
☐ Too Touchy ☐ Looney
☐ Other ______________________________

Appearance: ☐ Casual/Stylish ☐ Casual/Sloppy
☐ Polished/Professional ☐ Overpolished
☐ Dirtbag ☐ Hot! Hot! Hot! ☐ Severe
☐ Other ______________________________

Initial 'Blink' Reactions: ☐ Hmmm… ☐ Ugh!
☐ Hello Gorgeous… ☐ Run! ☐ Other _______

Pace(s) Observed: ☐ Slow ☐ Medium ☐ Fast
☐ Superfast ☐ Other ____________________

Eye Movements: ☐ Jittery ☐ Long Holds
☐ Up to Right ☐ Up to Left ☐ Back and Forth

Consistency Observed: Does this Possible's presentation match what you know about them?
☐ Yes, absolutely ☐ For the most part
☐ Not so much ☐ Not at all

Does this person do what they say and say what they do? ☐ Always ☐ Mostly
☐ Sometimes ☐ Eh… ☐ Never

Observer Analysis: Are you taking your time?
☐ Yes ☐ No, why not? _________________

Do you want to jump this person's bones, fix them, or fight them? ☐ Yes ☐ No ☐ Maybe

Overall TLS danger rating: ______________

Recommendations and comments:

____

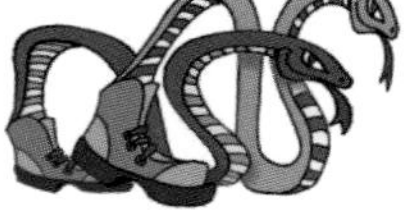

Two Legged Snake Spotters Checklist

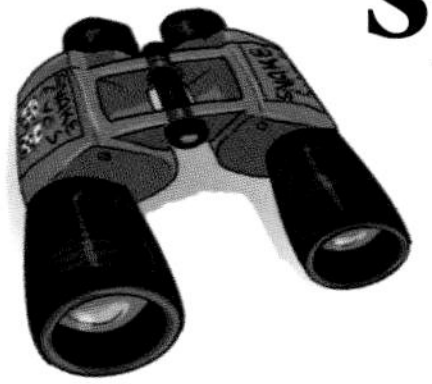
SNAKES
SNAKE

Possible Snake's Name/ID code: ______________

Observation Dates: ________________________

Social Level: ☐ D2D ☐ PBS

Possible Snake Types (Check all that may apply): ☐ The Charmer ☐ Backstabber
☐ Bombast Entertainer ☐ Bilker ☐ Decorated
☐ Misdirector ☐ Rhetorical ☐ Situational
☐ Media Maven ☐ Lost ☐ Lifer ☐ Justified
☐ King Cobra ☐ Transcendent
☐ Other (define attributes) ________________

Possible Fan Type: ☐ True Believer ☐ WannaBe
☐ Follow the Leader ☐ Loyalists
☐ Other (define attributes) ________________

Persauasive Techniques Observer:
☐ Accusination ☐ Misdirection ☐ Misassociation
☐ Going Big ☐ Disproportioning
☐ Rave-Up Questioning ☐ Burlesquing
☐ Bombasting ☐ Viperation ☐ Overtalking
☐ Demanding ☐ Begging Sympathy ☐ Flattery
☐ Yes Setting ☐ Reinventing History
☐ Other (define attributes)_________________

Biting Style Observed: ☐ The Nibbler
☐ The Chomper ☐ The Pouncer

Communication Style: ☐ Logical ☐ Rationalizing
☐ Passionate ☐ Pseudo-intellectual
☐ Bible Beater ☐ Hothead ☐ Leader ☐ Smarmy
☐ Too Polite ☐ Aloof ☐ Charming
☐ Too Touchy ☐ Looney
☐ Other ______________________________

Appearance: ☐ Casual/Stylish ☐ Casual/Sloppy
☐ Polished/Professional ☐ Overpolished
☐ Dirtbag ☐ Hot! Hot! Hot! ☐ Severe
☐ Other ______________________________

Initial 'Blink' Reactions: ☐ Hmmm… ☐ Ugh!
☐ Hello Gorgeous… ☐ Run! ☐ Other ________

Pace(s) Observed: ☐ Slow ☐ Medium ☐ Fast
☐ Superfast ☐ Other ____________________

Eye Movements: ☐ Jittery ☐ Long Holds
☐ Up to Right ☐ Up to Left ☐ Back and Forth

Consistency Observed: Does this Possible's presentation match what you know about them?
☐ Yes, absolutely ☐ For the most part
☐ Not so much ☐ Not at all

Does this person do what they say and say what they do? ☐ Always ☐ Mostly
☐ Sometimes ☐ Eh… ☐ Never

Observer Analysis: Are you taking your time?
☐ Yes ☐ No, why not? __________________

Do you want to jump this person's bones, fix them, or fight them? ☐ Yes ☐ No ☐ Maybe

Overall TLS danger rating: ______________

Recommendations and comments:

____

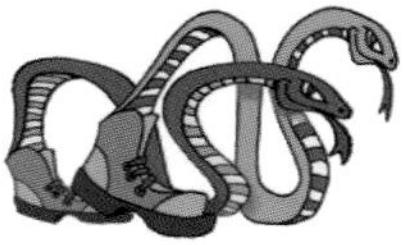

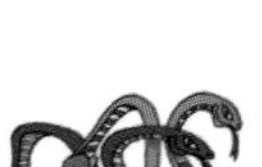